MW00583792

I GO TO THE RUINED PLACE:

*Contemporary Poems
in Defense of Global Human Rights*

I GO TO THE RUINED PLACE:

*Contemporary Poems
in Defense of Global Human Rights*

edited by

MELISSA KWASNY & M.L. SMOKER

LOST HORSE PRESS
Sandpoint, Idaho

I GO TO THE RUINED PLACE

Copyright © 2009 Lost Horse Press
Introduction © 2009 Melissa Kwasny & M.L. Smoker

Printed in the United States of America.

All rights reserved. No part of this book may be reproduced or transmitted in any form or by any means, electronic or mechanical, including photocopy, recording, or any information storage and retrieval system now known or to be invented, without permission in writing from the publisher, except by a reviewer who wishes to quote brief passages in connection with a review written for inclusion in a magazine, newspaper or broadcast.

Cover art: *Survivor,* 22" x 28" oil on canvas by Jun Cha, whose art may be viewed online at www.juncha.net

Melissa Kwasny's photo: John Sims

M.L. Smoker's photo: Sally Johnson

Book design by Christine Holbert

FIRST EDITION

This and other Lost Horse Press titles may be viewed online at www.losthorsepress.org.

LIBRARY OF CONGRESS CATALOGING IN PUBLICATION DATA

I go to the ruined place : contemporary poems in defense of global human rights / edited by Melissa Kwasny & Mandy Smoker. —1st ed.
        p. cm.
ISBN 978-0-9800289-7-3 (alk. paper)
1. Human rights—Poetry. 2. American poetry—21st century. I. Kwasny, Melissa, 1954- II. Smoker, M. L. (Mandy L.), 1975-
    PS595.H76I2 2009
    813'.60803554—dc22
                                2009044198

Publication of this book has been made possible by generous donations from the following Idaho human rights organizations and committed individuals:

The Benedictine Sisters of the Monastery of St. Gertrude • *Cottonwood, Idaho*

Bonners Books • *Bonners Ferry, Idaho*

The Bonner County Human Rights Task Force • *Sandpoint, Idaho*

Genevieve Campbell • *Sandpoint, Idaho*

The Employees of the East Bonner County Library District • *Sandpoint, Idaho*

Herta Feely • *Washington, D.C.*

Diana Gore & Shannon Barnes • *Sandpoint, Idaho*

Elsie & Richard Hollenbeck • *Bonners Ferry, Idaho*

Lanie Johnson & Ken Fischman • *Sandpoint, Idaho*

Kimberley Marshall • *Sandpoint, Idaho*

Wanda & Tom J. Newton • *Caldwell, Idaho*

Thomas Trusky • *Boise, Idaho*

Christopher White • *Sandpoint, Idaho*

TABLE OF CONTENTS

INTRODUCTION

IN OUR MEDIA-SATURATED LIVES, we are constantly aware of, and often desensitized to, the heinous violations of human rights occurring around the world. Yet the disclosures of U.S. sanctified torture at Abu Ghraib, at Guantanamo, and recently at the so-called 'black sites,' that system of secret prisons to which suspected terrorists were sent, has unsettled and profoundly disturbed many of us. In fact, much of our discomfort and awareness can be attributed to the permeation of media, especially in the form of the internet, into our daily lives and consciousness. Without YouTube, we would have never learned of Iranian martyr, Nedra, and her unfortunate death at a time when her country's government worked so diligently to keep all dissident information within its borders. Suddenly, as we become better informed about world-wide issues, our stake in them becomes much more acute.

More specifically, with the horrific photographs of Abu Ghraib, which were released to the public in 2003 and gained worldwide notoriety through the internet, and continuing through the release of the Red Cross Reports on the treatment of detainees in C.I.A. custody in February of 2007, we suddenly seem to be asked to decide to what extent we will stand up and speak out for human rights. It has become all too clear that none of us can take basic human rights for granted, whether our own or those of others affected by the actions of flawed and precarious governments.

Former President George W. Bush, whom Mark Danner quotes in his recent article, "U.S. Torture: Voices from the Black Sites," said, in referring to the Supreme Court ruling that states that we must conduct ourselves under the Common Article III of the Geneva Convention, "And that Common Article III says that, you know, there will be no outrages upon human dignity. It's like—it's very vague. What does that mean 'outrages upon human dignity?'" In fact, it is very clear what it means, despite euphemisms such as "alternative sets of procedures" and "enhanced interrogation techniques." The Geneva Convention, ratified by the United States, and upheld in the War Crimes Act of 1996, passed by the U.S. Congress, states that "willful killing, torture or inhuman treatment, including biological experiments, willfully causing great suffering or serious injury to body or health" is a serious breach of the Conventions.

When we made our call for submissions for an anthology of poems in defense of human rights, the allegations of torture were foremost in our minds. We knew people were outraged, saddened, profoundly moved and ashamed. But we also wanted to reach people who had suffered violations of their own rights from circumstances across the globe, or whose families had, or for whom preventing or healing these violations had become a life's work. We drafted our call loosely: *We are increasingly witness to torture, terrorism and other violations of human rights at unprecedented degrees. What do our instincts tell us and what is our response to these violations? What is our vision of a future wherein human rights are not only respected but expanded?*

What we received were both first hand accounts of violation—see prisoner Adrian English's "Raped Man's Stream of Consciousness," or Farnoosh Moshiri's poem recounting the terror of giving birth in Iran, or Li-Young Lee's "Self-Help for Fellow Refugees"—and responses from people who feel struck personally by the blows enacted on others: To speak for, to speak as, and to speak against. We were surprised at the range of issues spoken to by the poets. While torture remained a critical topic, as well as issues at stake in the Iraq War, there were also poems that addressed immigrant rights, prisoners' rights, the Holocaust, the wars in Cambodia, Vietnam, Serbia, South America, Palestine and Israel. We received poems that spoke of suicide bombing, violence against women, the aftermath of 9/11, and outlawing marriage for gay Americans.

We were also moved at the range of experience among the responders: homeless advocates, civil rights workers, clinical social workers, medics, the mentally ill, veterans, humanitarian aid workers, teachers, conscientious objectors, and, of course, many writers who work and fight daily for social justice in their communities. We are particularly proud of the number of Native American poets included in this anthology, something unusual in anthologies of this sort. It seemed to us impossible to collect a group of poems on human rights issues if we didn't acknowledge the far reaching and often appalling violations that have taken place in our own country, upon the first citizens of this land who belong to five-hundred-sixty-two federally recognized tribes who function as sovereign nations. It is the acknowledgement of this history, among others, that will allow us to move forward as a country with a clearer conscience, extending our hand to other nations and other peoples who continue to endure neglect and abuse.

This anthology could not exist without the courageous and important work of writers like Carolyn Forché, whose *Against Forgetting: Twentieth Century Poetry of Witness* first demonstrated the importance and power of poems that speak to the politics of our lives. Sam Hamill and Sally Anderson's *Poets Against the War* was a swift and strong response by poets to the current Iraq War. William Heyen's *September 11, 2011: American Writers Respond* is just one of many anthologies that speak to this indelible event. For those readers who would like to learn more about global human rights, the document written and approved by the United Nations on December 10, 1946, entitled *Universal Declaration of Human Rights* is profound in its clarity and beauty and yes, lack of vagueness.

Through all such interconnected efforts, by speaking, responding, acknowledging, and creating, we ensure first and foremost that the lives and legacies of those lost in the struggles to protect human rights will never be forgotten. We are witnesses, from all corners of the earth, from all walks of life, from one human being to another. We would like to express our appreciation, as fellow poets, for the courage and determination we must all display in order to originate work that represents the full spectrum of interactions, experiences, and reflections upon human rights issues. Many of us believe that a world built upon compassion and empathy truly is attainable—if not for us, then for future generations.

—*Melissa Kwasny & M.L. Smoker*

SANDRA ALCOSSER

THE BLUE VEIN

To be human is of the earth, crumbling

·

Is humus. Is humility. Bleeding

·

We fall down. A dog licks our blood. Sometimes

·

We eat songbirds because we are hungry

·

A poet might refuse to speak after

·

Shelling. Another sings until they starve

·

Him, not because he plots against the state

·

Because he makes his own song. For the way

·

She loved his music, and the way he loved

·

The blue vein that rivered from her eyebrow

·

To her brain, the widower on the pier

·

Lifts his cello. Wrist becomes lips, tongue

·

Casals played Bach each morning to sanctify

·

The house, sanctify the mind. We are all

·

Ephemerals. Our blood so close to the

Blood of a tree. The cello too is pine

·

A body with ribs, belly. Below the

·

Winter bud each genus grows its own face

·

Vedran Smailovic walks Sarajevo

·

With a cello. He wears a tuxedo

·

Skeleton of the body is the music's

·

Shape. *I don't think about bombs, about*

·

Snipers. We have to remind ourselves we

·

Are human. *I go to the ruined place.*

SANDRA ALCOSSER works for The Language of Conservation, a collaboration between scientists and librarians that supports sustainability of tribes and species. Her books, *A Fish to Feed All Hunger* and *Except by Nature,* have received many awards, including the James Laughlin from the Academy of American Poets, as well as awards from the Associated Writing Programs and the National Poetry Series. She is a member of the graduate faculty at San Diego State and Pacific University.

PETER ANDERSON

KEY TO THE KINGDOM

—for Phoenix Quin

The child has gleaming dark eyes, and a shy way
Of putting her head to the shoulder of the worried
Rescue worker, who tries to explain to camera
That the mother is dead, the father is dead, the gunmen
Unknown, but they shot up the party, the Christmas
Party, the same night I was at Carols by Candlelight
In the park with my children on my knees, and my wife
Said to me: "It takes you back to your own childhood,
Doesn't it?" As the Salvation Army raised
Their splendid brass in the rain, behind them
The lake, brilliant and dark with the lights shaking
Across it, and the minister, who strangely had
Exactly my name, proclaimed through the whoop
And whistle of a microphone that the child
In us held the key, the key to the kingdom,
And if only we would kneel with him there
And repent right then, he would guarantee us all
Peace on earth and goodwill to men. But the child
In me looks now at the child with gleaming eyes
Whose parents have been shot by "unknown assailants,"
And I know now that Christ was no better than
This child, and this world shall be changed for her sake.

PETER ANDERSON is South African. Opposed all his adult life to the apartheid régime, he was associated with an underground newspaper during the liberation struggle, and became a rank-and-file member of the United Democratic Front (UDF), which was indeed a front for Nelson Mandela's African National Congress while that party was still banned, in the 1980s. At present a professor of Postcolonialism and Creative Writing at Austin College in North Texas, Anderson has one collection of poetry, *Vanishing Ground*.

ELLEN BASS
BEARING WITNESS

—For Jacki Phoenix

If you have lived it, then
it seems I must hear it.

—Holly Near

When the long-fingered leaves of the sycamore
flutter in the wind, spiky
seed balls swinging, and a child throws his aqua
lunch bag over the school yard railing, the last thing,
the very last thing you want to think about
is what happens to children when they're crushed
like grain in the worn mortar of the cruel.

We weep at tragedy, a baby sailing
through the windshield like a cabbage, a shoe.
The young remnants of war, arms sheared and eyeless,
they lie like eggs on the rescue center's bare floor.

But we draw a line at the sadistic,
as if our yellow plastic tape would keep harm
confined. We don't want to know
what generations of terror do to the young
who are fed like cloth
under the machine's relentless needle.

In the paper, we'll read about the ordinary neighbor
who chopped up boys; at the movies we pay
to shoot up that adrenaline rush—

and the spent aftermath, relief
like a long-awaited piss.

But face to face with the living prey,
we turn away, rev the motor, as though
we've seen a ghost—which, in a way, we have:
one who wanders the world,
tugging on sleeves, trying to find the road home.

And if we stop, all our fears
will come to pass. The knowledge of evil
will coat us like grease
from a long shift at the griddle. Our sweat
will smell like the sweat of the victims.

And this is why you do it—listen
at the outskirts of what our species
has accomplished, listen until the world is flat
again, and you are standing on its edge.
This is why you hold them in your arms, allowing
their snot to smear your skin, their sour
breath to mist your face. You listen
to slash the membrane that divides us, to plant
the hard shiny seed of yourself
in the common earth. You crank
open the rusty hinge of your heart
like an old beach umbrella. Because God
is not a flash of diamond light. God is
the kicked child, the child
who rocks alone in the basement,
the one fucked so many times
she does not know her name, her mind
burning like a star.

A pioneer in the field of healing from child sexual abuse, ELLEN BASS first listened to the stories of survivors in the early 1970s; her work helped to transform not only the lives of survivors of abuse, but our societal awareness and understanding. She is co-author of *The Courage to Heal: A Guide for Women Survivors of Child Sexual Abuse,* which was revised for a 20th anniversary edition in 2008. Her poetry books include *The Human Line* (Copper Canyon Press, 2007) and *Mules of Love* (BOA Editions, 2002). She teaches in the M.F.A. poetry program at Pacific University.

JOSEPH BATHANTI

CLETIS PRATT

> And Samson said, Let me die with the Philistines.
>
> *—Judges 16:30*

First man I ever saw in irons, wearing nothing
but a pair of filthy white long john britches,
was Cletis Pratt, two guards, casually gripping
his upper arms, escorting him back to the population
after two weeks in single cell—same as the hole,
officially termed *Administrative Segregation.*
They had shaved his head.
He looked like Karl Marx.
He looked the wrath of Nazareth.
His big black beautiful beard was nappy and clotted
with what looked like lint, but he had gone grey in the hole,
and fat with outrage, eating thorazine and salt peter.
He'd never fooled around with weights,
had had a chiseled impossibly perfect onyx body,
where now pounded a gut and two silver dugs.
Hobbled by a short span of chain and two shackles,
another chain circling his waist to which his hands
were buckled, he couldn't quite keep up,
though the guards weren't hurrying him.
Sweating and winded, he bobbed and minced
like a dazed fighter—too exhausted to lift his heavy hands
to protect himself, to ask for mercy, to just go down—
his first day back in the gym, starting to train
again after a jolt in the penitentiary;

needles in North Charlotte;
needles on Hay Street in Fayetteville,
82nd Airborne, all the medals and insignia,
the Purple Hearts, his stunning beret.
Two tours in Vietnam.
Ten fucking lifetimes ago.

JOSEPH BATHANTI came to North Carolina as a VISTA Volunteer in 1976 to work with prison inmates. Since then he has taught creative writing in prisons, battered women's shelters and homeless shelters. He teaches at Appalachian State University in Boone, North Carolina. Bathanti is the author of four books of poetry: *Communion Partners, Anson County, The Feast of All Saints* and *This Metal,* which was nominated for The National Book Award. Star Cloud Press will publish his new collection of poems, *Restoring Sacred Art,* in 2010.

MARVIN BELL

BAGRAM, AFGHANISTAN, 2002

The interrogation celebrated spikes and cuffs,
the inky blue that invades a blackened eye,
the eyeball that bulges like a radish,
that incarnadine only blood can create.
They asked the young taxi driver questions
he could not answer, and they beat his legs
until he could no longer kneel on their command.
They chained him by the wrists to the ceiling.
They may have admired the human form then,
stretched out, for the soldiers were also athletes
trained to shout in unison and be buddies.
By the time his legs had stiffened, a blood clot
was already tracing a vein into his heart.
They said he was dead when they cut him down,
but he was dead the day they arrested him.
Are they feeding the prisoners gravel now?
To make them skillful orators as they confess?
Here stands Demosthenes in the military court,
unable to form the words "my country." What
shall we do, we who are at war but are asked
to pretend we are not? Do we need another
naive apologist to crown us with clichés
that would turn the grass brown above a grave?
They called the carcass Mr. Dilawar. They
believed he was innocent. Their orders were
to step on the necks of the prisoners, to
break their will, to make them say something

in a sleep-deprived delirium of fractures,
rising to the occasion, or, like Mr. Dilawar,
leaving his few possessions and his body.

MARVIN BELL'S nineteenth book is the wartime collection, *Mars Being Red* (2007). His most recent book is a collaboration titled, *7 Poets, 4 Days, 1 Book,* co-authored with poets from Hungary, Malta, Russia and Slovenia, as well as the U.S. (2009). For five years, he designed and led a ten-day workshop for teachers from the urban program, America SCORES. His poem, "The Dead Have Nothing to Lose by Telling the Truth," written for the University of Iowa's conference, "Global Focus: Human Rights '98," appeared in the USIA Human Rights booklet and in *The Future of International Human Rights,* edited by Stephen and Kathleen Marks.

TAMIKO BEYER

REPORT

A room just departed. The corners of a conversation. Struck.

The soldier knew what would become of it; she had been in long enough.

A stone thrown into the sky. An apostrophe. Left out not done not done
   not acted on but
abandoned not read aloud not at all read

but missing. Said-altered.

some things

were done

to a boy—

The first report marked well with the boy's gore. This one gone.
   Into no file no drawer no
military seal no stamp no stamp no paper stack.

She signed her name stamp stamped the second report thin and dry.
   Her still tongue as real as
the blister burned boy skin as real as.

Red welt rest. Easy not easy. Carry silence thick with the welt of it.

—burn cigarettes burn palm ear
shatter collarbone kick slash face
burn matches burn stomach crack
ribs kick puncture face burn
cigarettes burn forearm thigh
crack skull kick puncture stomach
burn cigarettes burn palm ear
shatter collarbone kick slash face
burn matches burn stomach crack
ribs kick puncture face burn
cigarettes burn forearm thigh
crack skull kick puncture stomach
burn cigarettes burn palm slash
ear face skull burn palm

TAMIKO BEYER divides her time between Brooklyn and St. Louis, where she is pursuing an M.F.A. at Washington University. Her poetry has appeared in *diode, Sonora Review, The Progressive* and other publications. She is a Kundiman Fellow and a founding member of Agent 409, a queer, multi-racial writing group that has led workshops across the country, including at the U.S. Social Forum, on ways to integrate creative writing with social justice work. She leads creative writing workshops for homeless LGBT youth, children from low-income families, and other communities.

MARK BRAZAITIS
THE POLICEMAN

Above me, suddenly, stood a policeman.

I was sitting under the tin roof of the *municipalidad*, waiting for the mayor, who was always expected, who rarely came. My bicycle was propped against the door of El Cuarto de La Niñez, the children's room, which was supposed to have powered milk and canned fruit; it was always locked. The policeman, his chest and stomach straining the blue threads of his uniform, began with pleasantries, and after he and I were done with our false-friendly exchange, he said, his voice casual, imperative, *"Prestame tu bicicleta."*

There were things I might have loaned a menacing stranger—money, my basketball, my Swiss Army knife.

But: *"Lo siento*, I don't lend my bicycle to anyone."

Undeterred, he demanded again—slowly, as if I hadn't understood.

One night, my friend Micaela, driving in Chamelco, was stopped by a pair of policemen. She didn't have a license. They said she could come with them to jail. Or she could touch them—touch them where they commanded. "No one," she told me, "wants to go to a Guatemalan jail. And they were only my hands." She held them up to me, small hands, the red nail polish faded. "They aren't pretty."

Policemen, every six months, work in a new town in the vicinity of their home base. I wondered about his last stop. Chamelco?

"I'm sorry—no."

He didn't say where he wanted to go with my bike; in his world, he didn't have to. His hand moved to brush his gun. Louder and with impatience: *"Prestame tu bicicleta."*

I didn't speak; worn down by his campaign and afraid, I didn't trust myself, this time, to say "No."

He grinned, a slow rising of his lips. "You treat it," he said, "like your lover. Is she good?" And he laughed, and I knew I was supposed to laugh, so I laughed.

He sauntered off.

It wasn't my victory. I came from a country with a thousand warheads in silos in Iowa and Montana, all this implied.

And, anyway, you ask, what would have been the harm in lending him my bike? He probably only wanted to ride down the street to say hello to Dolores, who always stood as thin as a half moon in the doorway of El Dragón.

A month later, he raped Blanca García, a student of mine, on the hill above her house. There were witnesses, her two little brothers, out to look for her in the dark. He had a choice: he could go to jail or propose marriage. That was the law. He offered; she refused.

He's still a policeman, someone told me. But he works in another town.

MARK BRAZAITIS is a former Peace Corps Volunteer and Technical Trainer and a founding member of the Appalachian Prison Book Project, whose mission is to put books in the hands of incarcerated women and men in Appalachia. An associate professor and the director of the Creative Writing program at West Virginia University, he is the author of *The Other Language,* winner of the 2008 ABZ Poetry Prize, and three books of fiction.

DONNA BROOK

POEM WRAPPED AROUND A QUOTATION FROM SAMANTHA POWER

It is strenuous to mentally
encompass events,
how much harder
to act on them.

Sunday bathers
lined the Jersey Shore as my stepson
cried for help from a riptide.
Alone my brother–in–law
dove and did not hesitate
to save him. Believed he could
and forthwith did, so becoming to us
a hero, no longer Sy,
but otherly brave.
Saying he did
what anyone would have done.

"To earn a death sentence, it was enough in the twentieth century to
be an Armenian, a Jew or a Tutsi. On September 11, it was enough
to be an American. In 1994, Rwanda, a country of just 8 million,
experienced the numerical equivalent of more than two World Trade
Center attacks every single day for 100 days. . . . When the Tutsi cried
out . . . every country in the world turned away."

But what would anyone
have done?

How demanding
to wrap the mind
around the Earth
as if plucking a drowning
man from the sea
because one conceives
it *is* possible.

The Tutsi were killed
with machetes and sharpened
car parts, means
of mass destruction,
just as water becomes
for those not snatched
from it in time.

DONNA BROOK, an associate editor of Hanging Loose Press, has published four collections of her poems and a history of the English language for children. A winner of NEA and NYFA fellowships for her poetry, she spent almost every night between the Democratic Convention and November 4, 2008 calling voters in New York, Pennsylvania and Ohio on behalf of Barack Obama. At present, besides working on poems, she is writing nonfiction prose about America's health care crisis.

A WOMAN CALLS

1.

Yesterday I went with the God of the dead to Kampala.
He pushed my face into dirt floors, cut me with a machete,
And smashed my head against doors.
I was made naked and a dim light raped me,
I was one woman lost, no more, I was a blood sponge in Uganda.

The sun went west, but no one in the tall buildings wrote down
    my death,
The traffic on white highways went to parking lots and malls,
And nothing changed at all.
But the air that I used to live in is leaving Africa,
And when my voice touches your lungs you will be less,
And when the air from many ending screams
Is a part of what you breathe, you will still be living
But your soul will be gone and you will be me.

2.

It is Sunday morning in early February,
The sun is lighting snow to white life,
Schubert is hovering over the coffee I drink black.
I like to read in a red chair, talk with my wife,
I like small pancakes in large stacks,
I don't comb my hair, I don't put on shoes,
I lay down, I don't look around, I am safe on my back.

3.

I count to thousands by hundreds,
The missing were once boys circling into soccer,
Parts of the sun and sun flower wild,
Now they are white with holes in their heads,
I think the murderers might take up my child,
I think of the full moon cut up and dead.

VICTOR CAMILLO is a mathematics professor at the University of Iowa. His short book, *The Disappeared,* was included in *New Poets, Short Books, Volume II,* edited by Marvin Bell and published by Lost Horse Press. The book focuses on past U.S.-supported right-wing terror in Latin America in the name of fighting the cold war.

LYNCH

not as in pin, the kind that keeps the wheels
turning, and not the strip of land that marks
the border between two fields. unrelated
to link, as in chain, or by extension whatever
connects one part to another, and therefore
not a measure of chain, which in any
case is less than the span of a hand hold-
ing the reins, the rope, the hoe, or taking
something like justice into itself, as when
a captain turned judge and gave it his name.
that was before it lost its balance and crossed
the border, the massed body of undoers
claiming connection, relation, an intimate
right to the prized parts, to the body undone.

MARTHA COLLINS is the author of the book-length poem, *Blue Front* (Graywolf, 2006), which focuses on a lynching her father witnessed when he was five, and which won an Anisfield-Wolf Award. She has also published four earlier collections of poems and two collections of co-translations of Vietnamese poetry. Her work with Vietnamese poets began at the William Joiner Center for the Study of War and Social Consequences in Boston, which she has been involved with for many years.

SARAH CONOVER

AGAIN, THE SERBS FAIL TO TAKE DUBROVNIK

> How evil all priesthoods.
> All over the earth Holy Places
> soaked with extra blood.
>
> —*Braided Creek*

In silver reliquaries, I count eleven finger segments
of nine saints. There must have been a frenzy
when they died, divided and carried away
to the cities of old Europe.
The oblate takes our money and leaves,
and now even breath seems too loud
in these stone cold rooms.
A saint's lips rest mute in a silver box.
Next, a handful of hair pressed under glass.
In the monastery courtyard, a single blade
of sun bleeds into the surrounding rooms.
Visiting here in 1929, George Bernard Shaw said,
"If you want to see heaven on earth, come to Dubrovnik."
This city, *the pearl of the Adriatic*, is painted on wall after wall,
as if claimed and reclaimed, and although
these frescoes reach from floor to ceiling,
it's impossible to see details under the war-blackened
glaze. Saints and bishops gauze the pigment's surface
as they bless the men and women of Croatia.
A partial skull rests on a shelf.
There are fresh graves just outside the city now.
New red roofs, and fresh stucco fill the bullet holes

that have bloomed around window frames during
the Serb siege. Only a month ago, when they left,
they scattered landmines on the hills to the east.
Here, they know that history belongs
not to the world's headlines, but to the places
where the dead hover close by, uncounted, expectant
of more. Outside, the streets of limestone singe our eyes
with Adriatic light, so we stay inside and wonder
how the dark remains so unyielding in these rooms.
Outside, they make fresh oaths knotting God with Croatia.
In here, there's an uneasy quiet, a silent incantation,
blood-darkened forearms. Skulls, fingers, vows.

SARAH CONOVER is the author of five books on world wisdom
traditions and spirituality. Her interests lie in building bridges between
cultures through her books, through working friendships with teachers
in Islamic countries, and through media she produced with the United
Nations and with *Internews*, a non-governmental agency dedicated to
open media around the world.

ROGER DUNSMORE

A TRUE WAR STORY

My friend's uncle
was a Marine in Korea.
His squad came to a cluster of huts,
smoke drifting up from one.
The squad leader ordered him
to go into that hut,
to kill everyone inside.
He stepped cautiously through the door
and waited for his eyes to adjust.
In the dim light he saw a terrified woman,
children huddled up against her.
He squeezed the trigger on his M-1,
emptied it into the thatched roof.
No one spoke
when he stepped back out
through that doorway.

Back home,
when he told the old people
what he had done,
they gave him a new name:
He-Who-Takes-Pity-On-His-Enemy,
and made him the Giver of Names
for new-born children.

ROGER DUNSMORE taught Humanities, Wilderness and Environmental Studies, and American Indian Literature at the University of Montana from 1963-2003. He presently teaches literature and writing at University of Montana, Western in Dillon. He has published three volumes of poetry and three chapbooks; edited *The Poetics of Wilderness* and *Put Sey' (Good Enough)*, poems by Victor A. Charlo. His *Earth's Mind: Essays In Native Literature*, 1997, was published by University of New Mexico Press. He has taught and led workshops at the Montana State Prison, Deerlodge; the Montana School For Girls, Helena; and at the Youth Correctional Center for Women in Boulder.

RAPED MAN'S STREAM OF CONSCIOUSNESS

As I stand on the threshold looking into darkness,
I wonder where you are and pray that you're still looking.
I'm not hard to find; just look for someone trying not to fall.
I sought you to redeem myself.
And yet I discovered that you weren't the saving type.
Honestly, you can be quite cruel.
And I wonder if that is a cruelty I can bear.
Wall upon wall has been brought down.
No new walls? Because I've run out of bricks.
And do you shun me because I'm exposed?
In a place of hard male virility, all life has been stripped away.
But to cope, I focus on a search outside of myself.
To rebuild inside, I pull from outside.
Inside, there is nothing left.
You believe yourself cruel, mean, nasty?
Imagine how I, a man scorned by everything, including his own intellect,
Would analyze you and break you apart.
Is it worth it to rebuild you?
I'm asking too many questions.
But, you've withheld too much.
I watch and I listen.
After all these times, I wonder if peace and happiness are meant to be had,
Or meant to be stolen.
I'm not afraid to be anguished.
If death is the ultimate beyond, then rape is the gateway.
And I'm at the other side of the door, still wondering
    how I got pushed through.
If you are already disturbed by my ranting,

Then I implore you to stop reading.
My carnival of nightmares is beginning.
In my sleep the event is repeated.
In my walking travails, I am suspicious.
You wear blue pants? I wonder about you.
You have a GDC number? I can't stand you.
And trust? There is no trust.
Love? That's that.
Every person I touch is poisoned.
Every time I reach out, my hand is swatted away as if I am a child.
Irony?
After the brutal taking of one's manhood,
There is nothing left but the child.
God bless the child

ADRIAN ENGLISH writes: "As a three time rape victim in prison, I am exposed to a violation of my human rights daily. It is not so much the act in itself but the attitude towards it. I get no help for my plight; I am pushed under a rug. How is it that our country decries others for their brutality when people like me exist inside our prisons. I'm not just a victim of rape, I'm a victim of justice. I write and draw because when you see my name, you see where I am, and you know what I've gone through. I'm not motivated by money or even a shot at freedom, I'm motivated by change. I was featured on *Hard-Times* (Channel. nationalgeographic.com/series/hard-time) and on *Top Shelf Comix* (www.topshelfcomix.com/ts2.0)."

CAROLYN FORCHÉ

THE MUSEUM OF STONES

These are your stones, assembled in matchbox and tin,
collected from roadside, culvert and viaduct,
battlefield, threshing floor, basilica, abattoir—
stones, loosened by tanks in the streets
from a city whose earliest map was drawn in ink on linen,
schoolyard stones in the hand of a corpse,
pebble from Apollinaire's *oui,*
stone of the mind within us
carried from one silence to another
stone of cromlech and cairn, schist and shale, horneblende,
agate, marble, millstones, ruins of choirs and shipyards,
chalk, marl, mudstone from temples and tombs,
stone from the silvery grass near the scaffold,
stone from the tunnel lined with bones,
lava of a city's entombment,
chipped from lighthouse, cell wall, scriptorium,
paving stones from the hands of those who rose against the army,
stones where the bells had fallen, where the bridges were blown,
those that had flown through windows, weighted petitions,
feldspar, rose quartz, blueschist, gneiss and chert,
fragments of an abbey at dusk, sandstone toe
of a Buddha mortared at Bamiyan,
stone from the hill of three crosses and a crypt,
from a chimney where storks cried like human children,
stones newly fallen from stars, a stillness of stones, a heart,
altar and boundary stone, marker and vessel, first cast, load and hail,
bridge stones and others to pave and shut up with,
stone apple, stone basil, beech, berry, stone brake,

stone bramble, stone fern, lichen, liverwort, pippin and root,
concretion of the body, as blind as cold as deaf,
all earth a quarry, all life a labor, stone-faced, stone-drunk
with hope that this assemblage of rubble, taken together, would become
a shrine or holy place, an ossuary, immoveable and sacred
like the stone that marked the path of the sun as it entered
   the human dawn.

CAROLYN FORCHÉ is a poet, translator and editor of the ground-breaking anthology, *Against Forgetting: Twentieth-Century Poetry of Witness*. A human rights activist for over thirty years, she was presented in 1998 with the *Edita and Ira Morris Hiroshima Foundation Award for Peace and Culture* in Stockholm for her work on behalf of human rights and the preservation of memory and culture. She has received fellowships from The John Simon Guggenheim Foundation, The Lannan Foundation and The National Endowment for the Arts. She has taught poetry and literature for thirty-five years, and holds The Lannan Chair of Poetry at Georgetown University, where she also directs The Lannan Center for Poetics and Social Practice.

GABE FURSHONG

REBURIAL

> Families have the right to exhume their dead,
> and this right should be guaranteed, given that the army was
> directly responsible for the vast majority of clandestine burials.
>
> —*The Recovery of Historical Memory Project, Guatemala*

A ring around the bone
was matched to a hand in the village.

Smaller skeletons were lying close
and togetherness had been the habit of their children.

Their bones were labeled.
Their bones were measured and scraped.
A finger was run inside a hole, along a split.

Five pine crates lie at the altar,
equally small and square.

A woman's breast slips from her hand-woven blouse,
her newborn swallows deep.

Church doors gape. Dust bends at the circle of men.

Five pallbearers shoulder the bones
like possessions boxed between houses.

Diggers pass them down easily,
a single round hole,
lighter than bundles of sticks.

Kneeling at the edge,
mothers old enough to be grandmothers.

Their voices waver.
Their thin voices gather a sequence.

GABRIEL FURSHONG writes from Helena, Montana where he
works as a community organizer on wilderness campaigns in western
Montana. He made five trips to Guatemala and southern Mexico
between 2000 and 2005 as a student and a volunteer for indigenous
rights organizations. "Reburial" documents a reburial that took place
in the state of Chimaltenengo, Guatemala in the fall of 2000.

KIM GOLDBERG

GATES OF THE CITY

This is the garden

This is the scattering of fallen pears
        browning in long grass

This is the closer glance, the tour bus
        kodak moment of the digitally captured herd
                asnooze on the savannah

These are the mounds of almost-
        life waiting for their time, over-ripened fetal
                curls quietly fermenting in spew of tailpipes

This is the new hope
        centre rising as leviathan across the highway

These are the jaws unhinging, swinging
        wide to passively consume the motile

These are the fourmilliondollar twentybeds
        offered freely to those who do not swear or have
                "bad conversations"

This is the little prayer
        they must all say, have all been saying since
                residential school days, small hands knotted
                    in fetal curls, in captured herds, their unhinged hearts
                        quietly fermenting in spew of charity

This is the scattering of fallen
        pears browning in long grass

These are the mounds of almost–life
        waiting for their time

This is the garden

The author of six books, KIM GOLDBERG'S poetry, prose and political writings have appeared in numerous magazines and anthologies in North America and abroad. Born and raised in Oregon, Kim moved to Canada with her family during the Vietnam War years and has remained in Nanaimo, B.C. ever since. As a journalist she has covered Native affairs extensively, including the plight of Native survivors of Canada's notorious church–run residential schools. "Gates of the City," from her *Red Zone* collection of poems, describes the vista upon entering downtown Nanaimo.

GRACE GRAFTON

MARS CONJUNCT URANUS
(OR, THE SAME OLD STORY)

The planets have aligned in explosives, instincts foment revamp, the drunk under the bridge cries foul. Birds themselves are blown off-course by the hurricane invading our capitol coast, the election to right all wrongs has been postponed by judges who sit on a bench most often overturned by human standards. And who are the standard bearers, who the beards marching to the beat of altars, of antics, of addicts? General men assign hysteria to the apron wearers, but who came up with the sword-waving intent to assassinate the premier? Not to say a kitchen woman wouldn't. Our dirty underwear shows again, flapping like raptor wings on the lines of overwhelmed minds. Some are being forced to kneel, others of us lay our bodies down on unroofed earth, pull fallen leaves over our arms, make love while the sky drops.

GRACE MARIE GRAFTON'S chapbook, *Zero*, won the Poetic Matrix Press contest. Her book, *Visiting Sisters*, was published by Coracle Books. Grafton considers her work in the California Poets in the Schools programs to directly promote human rights: "I am convinced that every child benefits from the right to express and develop themselves through making art. Additionally, through emphasizing nature poetry and conducting poetry field walks and writing garden poems, I expose students to Chief Seattle's idea that we belong to the earth, the earth does not belong to us."

JEREMY HALINEN

EARTH

From this disadvantage point, I point out
the gay gods' teeth planted in pathways
I will likely never walk with my hand
in the hand of another.
And what of the toothless gods? Do they ignore us,
their mouths full of what they traded their burning bones for? We
    worship
and still we die at the hands of men who hold hands with women
    and guns.

JEREMY HALINEN is a co-editor and co-founder of *Knockout Literary Magazine* (knockoutlit.org), which aims to further human rights by giving voice to LGBTQ authors, and by donating a portion of the proceeds of sales to nonprofit organizations, such as the Valentino Achak Deng Foundation, which provides educational opportunities to children in Sudan, and The Trevor Project, the United States' only nationwide, around-the-clock crisis and suicide prevention helpline for LGBTQ youth. He currently resides in Seattle.

SCOTT HIGHTOWER
RUBBER DOLLIE

> The only permanent thing is the soul,
> and what has happened to it.
>
> —*Patrick Kavanagh*

Like a dancer covered in nothing
but white powder, then sponged

with course brown makeup;
nothing else in plain sight

but silver anklets; arms
extended to take

the tribute of a guard's embrace.
We are watching from behind;

though, there are no flowers,
no curtain. And it's not a ballet.

It's a macabre charade,
one night in the secret

theater of Abu Ghraib.
The anklets are shackles.

In another, a leashed
dog—loud, black,

and snarling—takes
center stage. And, in others,

real men, looking like oddly
manipulated Kachina dolls

or naked degraded marionettes
in medieval hoods—

their elbows akimbo—
are paraded, strung erect,

wired, collapsed;
are stacked into a pile.

"Save us
from noisy oblivion;

from despair. Save us,
one by one,

from Roman cruelty;
from death

by water;
from death

by fire. Save us
from being eaten alive."

SCOTT HIGHTOWER'S third collection, *Part of the Bargain*, received the 2004 Hayden Carruth Award. His translations from Spanish have garnered him a Willis Barnstone Translation Prize. He is presently working on a set of poems focusing on the legacy of the Spanish Civil War and a non-fiction piece dealing with Tejano culture. He is also a long-time advocate of LGBT full civil rights. A native of central Texas, he lives and works in New York City.

CHRISTOPHER HOWELL

IF THE MOON KEPT GOATS:
THE VETERAN'S TALE

I can't believe I'm saying this
again after so many years, but those things that keep
coming back
name us
and we have to let them in.

There was a war.

Unquenchable roaring bells surrounded it
like a woman on fire inside a dress. Some of us
were taken away on ships to be part of this
and came back full of broken furniture, our faces
black kites over field of ice.
We had walked in harness so wrong and deep,
not even the sand man
would let us sleep.

And me? I was a case.

I left everything lie like dead thieves in a bank,
and, beyond loyalty and war, set my desperate bones
to hold a woman
who could barely hold herself
inside the world become a world
I didn't know.
And what if she had left her husband then
and the light by which we thought we knew

ourselves
had not failed, as it does, when we needed it
exactly?

What if the moon kept goats?

As I touched her to lure happiness out
of its tormented cage,
I thought of my father's faithfulness
and wondered how it was,
and by what right, he had returned from his
war and fashioned
from the remnants a whole life.

I thought of the southern cross and the enemy—then
now and always—looking up, as we had,
but breathing easy, minds luffing a bit, buoyed out
by the wonder of clarified commitment
and it occurred to me that from a certain point of view
there was no hope at all.

I saw things in the trees.
I stopped eating salt
and grew a red shadow which drifts with me
still under the April wood, circling
a candle of dead confusion, unable to blow it out.

Think of that.

Think of a whole generation of us, hands
in our fathers' hands

and the sun seething with impossible conjunctions, war
on both sides of us and love
in between.

CHRISTOPHER HOWELL'S ninth collection, *Dreamless and Possible: Poems New & Selected,* will be published by the University of Washington Press in 2010. His human rights concerns are keyed mainly against organized violence of all kinds, which *always* brings more suffering, one way or another, upon innocent civilians and unwilling combatants than upon those responsible for the action. He is a Vietnam-era veteran.

ELIZABETH MARTINEZ HUERGO

COMMON RENDITION

The old man stands in the heat of the sun,
remembering himself,
a political prisoner at *Boniato*,
every ache pressing, macerating his body,
forming phantom wings that seem to bud
then raise him, as he gazes east,
the city of Havana
spreading its delicate arc before him,
gently mocking the trajectory of a life stunted,
its promise always oddly receding.

> The way he remembered Pedro,
> whose heart imploded from hunger;
> or Miguel, bound to a wheelchair,
> dying by inches of gangrene;
> or Angel, slated for release,
> propped up before a firing squad instead.
> Or crazy Albertico who,
> set free after twenty-five years,
> disappeared on a rubber raft,
> pushing north into a dark gale.

The heat of the sun,
the old man, sinew and bone,
remembering himself
trussed and hanging naked,
prodded, struck, cut, and nearly drowned,
gazing no longer toward Fidel's prison,

where he had evacuated himself of the life he had known,
but toward *Guantanamo*, the eastern edge of his homeland,
a hollowness rendered by guile;
but a place of which no one could dispossess him.

> His heart ached differently for Josélito,
> of all, the one who had chosen his own path,
> secretly gathering the long strips of palm each day,
> tucking them around his waistband
> then braiding them at night,
> in the twilight of his cell,
> before he lay down on the cold, bare floor
> to tap the rhythms of old *boleros*
> against the damp cinder-block walls,
> the sound glistening hopefully in the darkness.

Looking east now,
every moment became the same,
and in that confluence the city was a river of time
disgorged, cutting across the walls of an ancient labyrinth
and revealing its secret:
the dull repetition of blood-soaked earth,
of stone recoiling with the cries of those
beaten, violated without mercy
in rituals that devolve when individual pathologies
are harnessed to a cause.

> Just a few days before the path
> opened before him,
> glistening like a crystal in his mind's eye,
> Josélito stopped eating the greasy soup,
> stopped tapping his beloved *boleros*,

or trying to imagine the time before *Boniato.*
He stopped everything
except the oddly arcing smile
that cut across his face
unconsciously.

Refracted through the lens of human cupidity,
the story arcs across centuries, cultures, causes.
The unrepentant are absolved,
aligned to a machine that filters, sorts,
claims the past for itself,
dictating the nobility of its torturers,
then enshrining them,
like the images of those children
drawn in pearl tones about the feet of a blue-eyed Christ,
more gladiator than scourged middle-eastern shepherd.

    The guards cut Josélito's body down,
    tossing it into the sea,
    leaving behind on the window grate
    the braided cord,
    simple detritus, supple and green,
    offered with humility once
    to soften the prophet's stony passage;
    the green strips that Josélito had braided together,
    thinking how he would shape
    the remaining arc of his life.

The old man could still hear Josélito's cinder-block boleros,
feel the comfort the sound had given him
in the depth of that nocturnal solitude.
He could feel the contours of the stolen land, too,

like the ribbed, brittle surface of the cord, Josélito's last gift,
which the old man carried with him so many years later.
Who would rise from the silent tombs of *Boniato* and *Guantánamo?*
What language would they speak?
The sound of the waves and the smell of the sea, the arc of the city;
they reminded him always of impossible loss, impossible hope.

E. M. HUERGO is a writer as well as Professor of English at Mont-
gomery College in Rockville, Maryland, where she teaches English
and American literature, Creative Writing and Women's Studies. Born
in Havana, Cuba, she came to this country as a political refugee.
In 1985 and 1989, she completed her M.A. and Ph.D. in 19th centu-
ry American Literature and British Romanticism at Brown Univer-
sity. Since 1983, she has taught at a number of institutions, including
Brown University, Rhode Island College, American University and
Montgomery College.

ANN HUNKINS

ONE DAY YOU WAKE UP

For years the anguish gets no answer. The given-up,
the heart-shattered, the shell-shocked have no place
to hide, their suffering frozen in an open field. Each human
body in the end to face embitterment, or not, alone,
and nothing can change what happened, nothing.

No help appears to the helpers, wondering if their help
helped anyone. If it helped the widow, to whisper on a rooftop
of her husband's killing. If it helped to rebuke slick-whiskered
Maoists, Army Captains and Generals. If it helped the illegally
detained, families of the disappeared, hunger strikers or the dead.

But one day you wake up and the sun is shining on the snow.
Suddenly the iron weight is off your chest. Nothing is changed.
The boy's head is still torn apart by a bomb. The husband is still forced
under and drowned. The months of beatings and shocks don't go away.
But for a moment it feels fresh, like being born again.

The sun and the snow. The brightness almost too much to stand.
A flicker startles at your doorstep. Rabbit prints all over the yard,
a looping criss-cross frenzy. Warmth. Snow sliding off trees,
pines lifting their branches, water running again, the earth turning
soft and muddy, permeable. Your hands, your feet under you.

You know it won't last. Still, it keeps coming back, like evening.
Like the moon, it looks a little different every time. Its slow flame
chars a path through the stars, the shards, the shivers, across
the broken heart-field, mine-field, the same one everywhere,
littered with socket-bombs, serenity, sorrow and solid earth.

ANN HUNKINS is a poet, photographer and translator of Nepali. A former Fulbright scholar with an M.A. in poetry from UC Davis, she is currently translating a Nepali novel into English on an NEA translation grant. She worked as a language interpreter for the United Nations Office of the High Commissioner on Human Rights in Nepal during the Maoist conflict in 2006, translating for war crimes witnesses, torture victims, and others. She currently writes and milks goats in Santa Fe, New Mexico.

LOWELL JAEGER

MAN

with cardboard sign.
Freeway exit.
In the rain.
Please.

We drive by and debate
right and wrong.

I watch the wipers.
Water. Human flesh
is water, mostly.

The globe is water, mostly.
Seas and oceans, co-mingle.
All currents, all depths.

Even this trickle
gathering at the roadside.
When we dip a finger
in the flow,
don't we touch
one body?

And when it rains,
doesn't it rain on us all?

LOWELL JAEGER teaches creative writing at Flathead Valley Community College in Kalispell, Montana. His poems are forthcoming in *The Iowa Review, Atlanta Review, The Coe Review, Poetry Flash, Georgetown Review, Big Muddy, Antioch Review, Louisiana Review,* and others. His third collection of poems, *Suddenly Out of a Long Sleep*, was published by Arctos Press in 2008. Currently Lowell Jaeger serves as editor of Many Voices Press and is busy compiling *New Poets of the American West*, an anthology of poets from Western states.

MATTHEW KALER

KALASHNIKOV STACCATO

> It made a roar like a train at night.
>
> —*James Joyce*

Darfur gaping. Alarm within.
The woman kept prisoner in a chicken coup
mouths the current etymology of her name, *lingua franca,* to the
 Western Man:
Nyanath in the time of pestilence,
her sheared dress billows.

Green militias in uniform wag AK-47s
like the threat of their genitals
or the gasoline soaked rag.
The residue of violence slinks her village ruins.

She pulpits the Western Man's subconscious. In his dream recurring
she squats inside a wire coup, building a wall from pebbles & mud
 & placebo
to keep back the Janjaweed.
He stands outside, considering the latch.

Both would agree on suffering as prostrating,
that it was first an act of rebellion: the body's
toward the mind, then mind toward the body.

Her hands are tiny against metallic sky.
The papers spiral like twisting ivory bodies,

make petulant roars at thought.
He promises to quiet the compassion fatigue.
She fuses her identity to *Nyanath* in exile,   to the alarm within.

Alarm. He wakes like a child
on a porch, the sky thick with magpies
& the question of appropriateness, the kitchen pornographic with jazz
opulence of croissants & newspaper.
He considers the story in print, words like grass waving in wind,
promises himself that this will be unlike those other mornings—

Over coffee-scent he revisits the dubious image—
a woman shuddering in a hutch for yard birds,

        made cavity
        handed meth & a razor
to rape the count of days into her arm, scar her censure,

where above her thousands of handwritten testimonies dart in air.

MATTHEW KALER is a member of *Savedarfur.org*. He is a graduate of the M.F.A. program at the University of Montana, Missoula, the city of his birth. The Sudanese name *Nyanath* means 'daughter of a human.' He writes, "After viewing a report on BBC World in which a Sudanese woman, held captive as a sex slave and forced into methamphetamine addiction, returned to her village and built a tiny wall around her hut, hoping to protect her children if the Janjaweed returned, I was compelled to write this poem. I can do more, and remind myself of this daily. But most important is the coupling of the reminder with an action. I deeply hope that poetry, as a branch of the arts, can constitute such action."

ILYA KAMINSKY

WE LIVED HAPPILY DURING THE WAR

And when they bombed other people's houses, we

protested
but not enough, we opposed them but not

enough. I was
in my bed, around my bed America

was falling: invisible house by invisible house by invisible house.

I took a chair outside and watched the sun.

      In the sixth month
of a disastrous reign in the house of hands

in the street of hands in the city of hands in the country of hands
our great country of hands, we (forgive us)

lived happily during the war.

ILYA KAMINSKY was born in Odessa, former USSR, and arrived in the United States in 1993 when his family received asylum from the American government. In the late 1990s, he co-founded Poets for Peace. His book, *Dancing in Odessa* (Tupelo Press, 2004), was awarded the Dorset Prize, a Ruth Lilly Fellowship from *Poetry* magazine, the Whiting Writers Award and a Lannan Fellowship. It was also named the Best Poetry Book of the Year by *ForeWord* magazine.

MOHA KAHF

ASIYA'S ABERRANCE *(NUSHUZ ASIYA)*

> O my Lord, build for me a house near You in the Garden,
> and save me from Pharoah and his doings
> and save me from the people who oppress.
>
> —*Prayer of Asiya, surrogate mother of Moses. Quran, Forbiddance: 11*

These chariot horses are flying from me.
The world hurtles by at frightening speed:
Bodies explode in mid-air.
Pyramids come crashing down into dust.
Children are deliberately slaughtered.
Homes with people living in them are demolished.
Prisoners, hooded naked, are dog-leashed
in the name of freedom.
Journalists, bound, are beheaded
in the name of truth.
People use the altars of the gods
to pray for killing.

I don't understand this world.
I want to build myself a house
in another sort of world.
I wake from one of my nightmares.
Pharoah says, "Why are you screaming?
You have everything you ever wanted.
We live like kings." Then he laughs, turns into
a river of blood, a serpent crawling up my thigh.
I am splayed unclothed across a billboard.

A book I love is shoved into a toilet.
The nightmare isn't over, isn't over.

The priests of state pray loudly for victory.
They turn into frogs, make disgusting noises,
look at me warily. The scholars and the teachers
explain why I am wrong
according to the laws
everybody knows.
The newspapers call me crazy woman, lesbian,
traitor to the country, fascist, anarchist,
an apologist for terrorists, an apostate to the faith—

but it's Pharoah who's crazy.
It's this upside-down order of yours
that endangers the country.

It's the gods that accept
libations for murder
who are crazy.

Got to hold on
to these snorting horses.
Got to get the reins back
or they will break my neck.
I'm going over—
I'm going over—
But not because I'm crazy.

MOHJA KAHF was born in Damascus, Syria and is an associate professor of Comparative Literature at the University of Arkansas. Her books include a novel, *The Girl in the Tangerine Scarf* (Perseus, 2006), a book of poetry, *E-mails from Scheherazad* (University Press of Florida, 2003), and a book of scholarship, *Western Representations of the Muslim Woman* (University of Texas, 1999). She has lived in the Arab world and returns there regularly. Her study of early Muslim women, "Braiding the Stories: The Eloquence of Women in Early Islam" appears in Gisela Webb's *Windows of Faith: U.S. Muslim Women Scholar Activists*.

YUSEF KOMUNYAKAA

SURGE

Always more. No, we aren't too ashamed to prod celestial beings
into our machines. Always more body bags & body counts for oath
   takers
& sharpshooters. Always more. More meat for the gibbous grinder
& midnight mover. There's always someone standing on a hill, half
   lost
behind dark aviation glasses, saying, If you asked me, buddy, you
   know,
it could always be worse. A lost arm & leg? Well, you could be stone
   dead.
Here comes another column of apparitions to dig a lifetime of
   roadside graves.
Listen to the wind beg. Always more young, strong, healthy bodies.
   Always.

Yes. What a beautiful golden sunset. *(A pause)* There's always that
   one naked soul
who'll stand up, shuffle his feet a little, & then look the auspicious,
   would-be gods
in the eyes & say, Enough! I won't give another good guess or black
   thumbnail
to this mad dream of yours! An ordinary man or woman. Alone. A
   mechanic
or cowboy. A baker. A farmer. A hard hat. A tool-&-die man.
   Almost a smile
at the corners of a mouth. A fisherman. A tree surgeon. A
   seamstress. Someone.

YUSEF KOMUNYAKAA was born in Bogalusa, Louisiana, where he was raised during the beginning of the Civil Rights movement. He served in the United States Army from 1969 to 1970 as a correspondent and managing editor of the *Southern Cross* during the Vietnam war, earning him a Bronze Star. His book *Dien Cai Dau* (1988) has been cited as being among the best writing on the war in Vietnam. Since then, he has published many books of poems, including, most recently, *Warhorses,* and *Neon Vernacular: New & Selected Poems, 1977-1989* for which he received the Pulitzer Prize. He lives in New York City where he is currently Distinguished Senior Poet in New York University's graduate Creative Writing program.

CHRISTI KRAMER

THE RECALLER. THE RECKONER.
THE EFFACER OF SINS. THE WITNESS.

Knowing the tribal leader loved people who fear God and received
    priests graciously

                           whatever time they called,

the president had bombs sewn into the clothes of two priests.

                   The priests went about their day, unaware.

The president's secret service, counting on traditional seating order:
    priest, leader, priest,
sat across the street and, with fat thumbs, detonated the flax, never-
    dirtied robes.

Only the tea man got in the way, stepped in between.

        Glass, gold flecked glass, coal, fractured sugar cube, sliver of
    gold spoon, bird from
the pattern on the rug set loose, prayer beads unstrung, heart, morsel
    of date, no sound,
a window, a window, stream of cascading tea—bent bowing, light.
Silver serving tray rolled away.

CHRISTI KRAMER is a graduate of George Mason University's M.F.A. program, and currently a student in the Language and Literacy Education Ph.D. program at the University of British Columbia. Her poem, "The Recaller . . ." is from *Reading The Throne*, a book of poetry based on ethnography of Iraqi Kurds living in exile in Harrisonburg, Virginia. Kramer is the facilitator of the refugee Children's Writing Circle that presented "Iraqi Children Speak" at the Split This Rock Poetry Festival in Washington, DC, in March 2008.

MARILYN KRYSL

TARGET

When I look at the photo of Hamed, boy whose skull
keeps growing—when I look into those eyes
that can't close—the iris of Hamed's eye is the center
of the target at my uncle's shooting range. I
was eight when he took me into that force field,
bullets lined up in ranks. A man polished
his gun, I thought of a duck's feathery down,
then another shoved him, just kidding, jostling,
pressure in the cooker rising, and there was the downy
fuzz on my arm, tiny hairs available for harm.
Then my uncle raised his rifle, and his body let loose
the way, when the gate lifts, the stuck bull charges.
He'd hit the target's center, and then thrust the gun
over his head and leapt up and whooped. I knew
then that the world was dangerous, soft things

were in danger. Now I'm older, here morning's
pastel, the fractal branching of a tree, birds
twitter and coo, and I look into Hamed's eyes
and think of my daughter's body held close to my body,
myself looking out from that other photograph
the way the mother of Hamed looks out. I told
myself I would learn to run fast, and if they caught me
I'd turn and spit and scratch, and I would burn
a ring around myself with my fierceness, those flames
would burn them, I would be that angry. As now
I set fire to the ring I would burn around all children,
around the body of Hamed whose eyes stay open,
whose eyes, even after his death, will stay open.

MARILYN KRYSL has published four short story and six poetry collections. *Dinner with Osama* won the Richard Sullivan Prize in 2008, and *Swear the Burning Vow: Selected and New Poems* appeared in 2009. She has served as Artist in Residence at the Center for Human Caring, volunteered with Mother Teresa's Sisters of Charity in Calcutta, and worked as an unarmed bodyguard for Peace Brigade International in Sri Lanka. In Boulder she has volunteered with the Lost Boys of Sudan, and co-founded C-SAW, the Community of Sudanese and American Women.

LI-YOUNG LEE

SELF-HELP FOR FELLOW REFUGEES

If your name suggests a country where bells
might have been used for entertainment

or to announce the entrances and exits of the seasons
or the birthdays of gods and demons,

it's probably best to dress in plain clothes
when you arrive in the United States,
and try not to talk too loud.

If you happen to have watched armed men
beat and drag your father
out the front door of your house
and into the back of an idling truck

before your mother jerked you from the threshold
and buried your face in her skirt folds,
try not to judge your mother too harshly.

Don't ask her what she thought she was doing
turning a child's eyes
away from history
and toward that place all human aching starts.

And if you meet someone
in your adopted country,
and think you see in the other's face

an open sky, some promise of a new beginning,
it probably means you're standing too far.

.

Or if you think you read in the other, as in a book
whose first and last pages are missing,
the story of your own birthplace,
a country twice erased,
once by fire, once by forgetfulness,
it probably means you're standing too close.

In any case, try not to let another carry
the burden of your own nostalgia or hope.

And if you're one of those
whose left side of the face doesn't match
the right, it might be a clue

looking the other way was a habit
your predecessors found useful for survival.
Don't lament not being beautiful.

Get used to seeing while not seeing.
Get busy remembering while forgetting.
Dying to live while not wanting to go on.

Very likely, your ancestors decorated
their bells of every shape and size
with elaborate calendars
and diagrams of distant star systems,
but with no maps of scattered descendants.

·

And I bet you can't say what language
your father spoke when he shouted to your mother
from the back of the truck, "Let the boy see!"

Maybe it wasn't the language you used at home.
Maybe it was a forbidden language.
Or maybe there was too much screaming
and weeping and the noise of the guns in the streets.

It doesn't matter. What matters is this:
The kingdom of heaven is good.
But heaven on earth is better.

Thinking is good.
But living is better.

Alone in your favorite chair
with a book you enjoy
is fine. But spooning
is better.

LI-YOUNG LEE was born in 1957 in Jakarta, Indonesia, to Chinese parents. His father had been a personal physician to Mao Zedong while in China, and relocated the family to Indonesia, where he helped found Gamaliel University. In 1959, the Lee family fled the country to escape anti-Chinese sentiment and after a five-year trek through Hong Kong, Macau, and Japan, they settled in the United States in 1964. Lee is the author of *Behind My Eyes* (Norton, 2008); *Book of My Nights* (2001), winner of the 2002 William Carlos Williams Award; *The City in Which I Love You* (1991), the 1990 Lamont Poetry Selection; and *Rose* (1986), which won the Delmore Schwartz Memorial Poetry Award.

JOEL LONG
TAKING DOWN THE HOUSE

In a village in Pakistan, the mother lifts
stones, uncarved birds, stumps of hands,

lifts stones that smoke, exhale puffs
of dust from a mouth of mortar and block,

lifts stones above cloth, camouflaged
against stone, pant leg, shoe. Her son is a stone.

Go inside when the wind blows, she told him.
Go inside. Her son is a stone. His teeth

spill in her hands like rice. Her son is God.
She does not recognize him. She lifts stones,

his hand like cold tar when frost comes,
lifts, bringing the floor light, bringing dust,

radio, dead of voices, the speaker cone torn.
Go inside when the wind blows. Go inside.

The wind is blowing now.
The wind is blowing now.

JOEL LONG'S book, *Winged Insects,* won the White Pine Press Poetry Prize. His chapbooks, *Chopin's Preludes* and *Saffron Beneath Every Frost*, were published by Elik Press. His poems have appeared in numerous journals, including *Interim, Isotope, Gulf Coast, Rhino, Bitter Oleander, Crab Orchard Review, Karamu, Bellingham Review, Sou'wester, Prairie Schooner* and *Willow Springs,* and anthologized in *American Poetry: The Next Generation, Essential Love* and *Fresh Water.*

ADRIAN C. LOUIS

I THOUGHT I SAW DICK CHENEY CHASING A BUS IN MINNEAPOLIS

I thought I saw Dick Cheney
chasing a bus in Minneapolis.
He looked just like himself &
was wearing baggy new Levi's
with one of those chain things
hooked to a belt loop & then to
his wallet & God I'd never wear
such a gizmo as this old bastard
who was huffing & puffing through
traffic unaware his head was nearly bald
& his ponytail was constructed of neck hair.
I wanted to sneak up & ask if he were fatally
worn out from fucking his beloved country,
ask if he had enjoyed playing the player, but
he jumped on the bus & was gone, gone, gone.

ADRIAN C. LOUIS is a Professor of English in the Minnesota State University system. His 2006 collection of poems, *Logorrhea* (Northwestern University Press), was a finalist for the *Los Angeles Times* Book Prize. He is a former journalist and has been editor of four tribal newspapers, including the *Lakota Times* and *Indian Country Today*. He is an enrolled member of the Lovelock Paiute Indian Tribe.

PETER MARCUS

WORLD MUSIC

After midnight, Saigon, inside *Apocalypse Now.*
A bar-girl wearing cheap spandex brandishes a pool stick,
flirting with her newfound mates from Melbourne.
                            The barstools
are all occupied by lithesome, talc-faced girls
decked out in flaming hot pants or old world Chinese silks.
They glance from time-to-time at their imitation Swatches
as if waiting for an airlift to a milk-and-honey nation.
                            Over rounds
of ice cold Heineken, a clan of shit-faced travelers discuss
their recent visit to the War Remnants Museum, though no one
cares to mention shell casements in the countryside
converted into planters for eggplants, scallions and tomatoes.
                            My friend,
it's a brand new century. Whichever way you wander
you'll meet a limbless beggar while the music of Madonna,
Dire Straits and Sting pours onto the night time streets.
                            Beat your swords
into ploughshares, slip your condoms on. It's closing time.
Last dance. Last call.
The DJ spins. The patrons sing: *WE-ARE-FAMILY! WE!*

PETER MARCUS currently works as an Assistant Professor of Social Science at Borough of Manhattan Community College/City University of New York. His interest in human rights developed from work in multi-cultural psychology in the early 1990s while interning at Northern Arizona University in Flagstaff. He has been a member of Doctors Without Borders, Human Rights Watch, Amnesty International, the Carter Center, and other organizations that seek to address and rectify these inequalities and injustices. His manuscript, *Dark Square,* has been a finalist for several prizes, including the National Poetry Series.

PHILIP MEMMER

WATCHING THE BABY SLEEP

As each just-audible breath
lifts the small weight of his chest

a militiaman's bayonet
throws him into a ditch.

And as each sweet blanketed foot
gives a light and dream-slow kick

the older child beneath him
struggles for air.

Don't call this metaphor.
The bullets slip into them,

then out. As the soldiers turn
I reach down into his crib,

stroke the curve of his crown.
A miracle, this sleep,

when they are so many,
and their song is so loud.

PHILIP MEMMER is the author of three books of poems: *Lucifer: A Hagiography* (Lost Horse Press, 2009), *Threat of Pleasure* (Word Press, 2008) and *Sweetheart, Baby, Darling* (Word Press, 2004). He lives in upstate New York, where he directs the Arts Branch of the YMCA of Greater Syracuse and the YMCA's Downtown Writers' Center.

PHILIP METRES
LETTER TO MY SISTER

Katherine, when you came back
to our oak and maple suburb,
unreal, occupied, you caressed an olive tree
pendant, talked of ancestral homes

bulldozed for settler roads, olive groves
torn from the ground, your Palestinian love
unable to leave, his passport denied
at the airport. He'd never tell what he did

to be detained, words that could be taken
against your will. Instead, he gave you
this olive tree to hang around your neck,
said *a country is more important*

than one person. I don't know.
I've read emails of the new torture—
an overhead projector behind a prisoner,
turned on, until he feels his head

will catch fire. Last week, over baklava
and tea, rain pounding the door,
"Ashraf" spoke of barbed wire, boycotts
and curfews—how his dozen siblings split

into sides. *Israeli soldiers*
hurt you, and we wanted them to hurt.

We couldn't imagine any other way.
I wrote his story down. We met

again. He said I still didn't understand.
He said, *write me out, keep only*
the general outline, not how I slipped
through checkpoints or where I hid

when they came for us. What I wrote or said,
each revealing detail, could spell
someone's end. When the story appeared
in the *Voice*, he only ghosted its margins, shadow

to a place not fully his. But there's no story
without particulars. What resistance could live
on the stale bread of statistics, the drought
of broken accords? It almost requires

bloodstained walls of a mosque,
prostrate backs shot through—a visible sign
of an invisible disgrace. Today, I open
the newspaper, try to peer between the grain

of a photo: a staggering crowd, arms entwined
and straining, as if to hold something back.
It could be us, facing a danger constantly
off-screen. No, we were born here.

On the stove, potatoes boil.
NPR segues labor strike
and missile strike with witty violin.
Twilight, I'm looking out the window,

trying to strike a few words
into flame. The dark lowers its wet sack,
then hoods the whole house. Outside,
something is falling. I strain to see it

past the glare of the kitchen light.

PHILIP METRES is the author of numerous books, including *To See the Earth* (2008), *Behind the Lines: War Resistance Poetry on the American Homefront Since 1941* (2007), and *Come Together: Imagine Peace* (2008). He has worked for peace, social justice and human rights since the 1980s; he co-founded the Bloomington Coalition for Peace (Bloomington, Indiana) in the 1990s, and has worked with Amnesty International, Pax Christi, Cleveland Non-Violence Network, Committee for Peace in the Middle East, Peace Action, and Tikkun. He is an associate professor of English at John Carroll University in Cleveland, Ohio.

TIFFANY MIDGE

AFTER VIEWING THE HOLOCAUST MUSEUM'S ROOM OF SHOES AND A GALLERY OF PLAINS' INDIAN MOCCASINS: WASHINGTON, D.C.

The portrait is clear:
one is art, the other evidence.
One is artifact
the other atrocity.
Each is interned
behind glass,
with diagrams
and panels,
a testament to miles
walked. Both
are worn,
each a pair,
one is cobbled
one is beaded.

At my tour's end
can I buy a key-chain shoe?
Will I be assigned
the ID card
of one of the perished
at Wounded Knee?

The moccasins
are beautiful. Seed pearls
woven intricate as lace.

We don't mourn
the elegant doe skins,
we admire the handicraft.
We don't ask from whose soles
do these relics come from?
We don't look for signs of resistance,
or evidence of blood.

Nor do we wonder
if he was old
and passed in his sleep,
or if this child
traded for a stick of candy
or a pinch of dried meat.
We do not make assumptions
of original ownership at all.

Their deaths were not curated,
not part of an installation. We
don't absorb their violent
and harrowing ends under soft
lights or dramatic shadows.

We look right
through them,
more invisible
than the sighs
of ghosts.
And then we move
on to the next
viewing,

and the next,

and the next,

to another
collector's trophy
lying beneath
a veil of glass.

TIFFANY MIDGE is the recipient of the Diane Decorah Poetry Prize from the Native Writers Circle of the Americas for her collection of poetry, *Outlaws, Renegades and Saints: Diary of a Mixed-Up Halfbreed*, published by Greenfield Review Press, 1994. She has also authored a chapbook, *Guiding the Stars to their Campfire, Driving the Salmon to their Beds*, from Gazoobi Tales Press, 2005, and is a recent graduate of the University of Idaho's M.F.A. program.

JUDITH MONTGOMERY

SIMMER

Bent above the scarred desk, I aim
to limn the long pure streak of white

that cuts through egg-blue dawn,
the birches' lace-serrated shadow

as leaves begin to knuckle under
to October—but at eye's edge,

in my safe room's shadows, lurk
the leash, the bitter wire, the hood

that shimmers out of other shade . . . *Not
I,* I think. But the bleak objects insist:

they summon the stained chair, the socket
jammed with wrenched light, the gasp

of electricity that simmers in the wall's
innocent plug. Common objects. Rope.

Wire. Match. Knife. Waiting ready-to-
hand in every everyday American home . . .

I too can insist on innocence. That I not
be held accountable for skewed use. *Other*

users heft these tools in sweaty, sand-stung
palms, considering how each might best

be turned to terror . . . Now I've said it: how
fear deforms object. Subject. How it twists

the blessing of stout wire tight about
the most delicate of human parts. How

the honed blade edges into flesh, leaving
scarlet glyphs carved on body. Beyond.

How the chair comes to weep its litany
of piss and blood. How the young girl

who crouched frightened in the belly
of the stripped cargo plane, how in her

mottled regulation camouflage she steps
from shadow into sun. How she cuts

the next hood from a pattern frayed with use.
How the stripped wire warms in her

recruited hands. How before me she tests
the human leash lightly in her palm . . .

I open mine. The twisted rope burns.

JUDITH H. MONTGOMERY'S poems appear in *Bellingham Review*, *Ars Medica*, *Northwest Review*, *Cider Press Review*, and elsewhere. Her chapbook, *Passion,* was awarded the 2000 Oregon Book Award. *Red Jess,* her first full-length collection, appeared in 2006; *Pulse & Constellation*, a finalist for the Finishing Line Press Chapbook Competition, appeared in 2007. Her poetry of witness springs often in response to media photographs: moving through the interconnection of subject and artistic composition to focus on both the moral stance/ involvement of the photographer and the complicity of the viewer.

FARNOOSH MOSHIRI

BLOSSOMS CULLED, UNRIPE

I wake with a whistle in my head
A long shriek
Stitches the sky to earth
A bomb

I drive through the blue morning mist
A woman sobs in the radio
Her eight year old
Dies of breast cancer
In a hospital in Baghdad

All these blossoms culled, unripe—

Today is February the twenty-fifth
In a maternity ward
In the center of Tehran
In 1981
I died once
Giving birth to my son

There was no doctor
And the ward was filled with mutilated soldiers
A rude assistant nurse
A devotee of the Holy One
Called me "Infidel," "The Corrupter of the Earth!"

"You're just giving birth, shame on you!
Our brothers are martyred

Of the Holy War
Swallow your pain, woman
This is a war
Against Satan!"

A long whistle
Stitches the sky to earth

My sister laments in Baghdad
"Your blossoms uprooted
                              Gone
                                        My child—
What have we done to you, America?
What is our crime?

I drive through the blue morning mist
This is February the twenty-fifth
Two thousand and three
Do I have a present for my son?

A whistle in my head
A long shriek
A bomb

"What have we done to you, America?
My child is gone
Blossoms uprooted
                    Culled
                              Unripe!"

FARNOOSH MOSHIRI is an Iranian-born writer with three novels, one collection of stories, and many essays and poems published in the U.S. She was a writer and activist in Iran when the Islamic regime arrested, tortured and executed the secular intellectuals in the early '80s. In 1983 she went into exile with her two-year old son, crossing the border of Iran, entering Afghanistan. She lived for more than three years in Kabul, where she taught at the Kabul University. Again, in danger of being captured and killed by the Islamic Mojahiden, who were sponsored by the U.S. government, she moved to India as a refugee of the United Nations. In 1987 she emigrated to the U.S. and changed her creative language to English to reach a wider audience.

TRANSLATED BY CAROLYNE WRIGHT

TASLIMA NASRIN

NOORJAHAN

They have made Noorjahan stand in a hole in the courtyard,
there she stands, submerged to her waist with head hanging.
They're throwing stones at Noorjahan,
those stones are striking my body.

Stones are striking my head, forehead, chest and back,
they're throwing stones and laughing aloud, laughing and
   shouting abuse.
Noorjahan's fractured forehead pours out blood, mine also.
Noorjahan's eyes have burst, mine also.
Noorjahan's nose has been smashed, mine also.
Through Noorjahan's torn breast, her heart has been pierced,
   mine also.
Are these stones not striking you?

They're laughing aloud, laughing and stroking their beards,
there are *upis* stuck to their heads, they too are shaking with laughter.
They're laughing and swinging their walking-sticks;
from the quiver of their cruel eyes, arrows speed to pierce her body,
         my body also.
Are these arrows not piercing your body?

TASLIMA NASRIN was born in Mymensingh, Bangladesh, in 1962. In the late 1980s, she emerged as a poet, columnist, and fiercely independent feminist, renowned for her bold public criticisms of Bengali society and the Islamic religion, especially with regards to the attitudes toward and treatment of women. In 1989, for the *Dhaka* news magazine, she began to write columns commenting on social and gender issues such as *purdah*, prostitution, domestic violence, and female sexual oppression. In 1991, a collection of these columns, *Taslima Nasriner Nirbacita Kalam*, (*Selected Columns of Taslima Nasrin*), was published in *Dhaka;* the following year, it received the prestigious Ananda Prize, one of West Bengal's highest literary honors.

SHERYL NOETHE

NO EXCHANGE OF LIVESTOCK

It took me fifty years
        and countless attempts
to have normal sex.

No booze, no sedatives, no chemical euphoria,
        no alcoholic black-out.
No disassociating. No nearly dead drunk.

No "Can't remember" or if I ever said "No," or "Stop."
        No broken marriages. No betrayal, no danger.
No despair, no fixed silence. No blood. No infection.
        No lying, no secrets, no night terrors.
No choking or gagging, no warnings, no threats.
        No suffocation.

No brothel. No money. No blood feud.
        No exchange of livestock, no force.
No genital mutilation. No child brides. No angry God.
        No gang rape.
No dawn to dusk curfew. No chattel. No vessel.

No choice. No chance.
        And where was God?

They say God saved the few he could.
        The rest, however, he kept.

SHERYL NOETHE'S books include *The Descent of Heaven Over the Lake* (New Rivers Press, 2000), *The Ghost Openings* (Grace Court Press)—which won the William Stafford Award for Poetry and the Pacific Northwest Booksellers Award—a teaching text entitled, *Poetry Everywhere* (Teachers & Writers Collaborative Press), and most recently, *As Is* (Lost Horse Press, 2009). She is the founder of the Missoula Writing Collaborative in Montana which creates writers-in-residence opportunities in schools and outlying areas. Her life's mission is to "give children the chance I got when a 5th grade teacher told me I would be an author, thus giving me the ability to re-write my (miserable) life."

BEIRUT

The boy drags himself along on a piece of cardboard all day,
a coffee can in front of him, old slippers over his hands,
    pulling himself on
with the friction of his own weight, this morning up Hamra street,
people hurry to work, stepping over small craters, cracks and holes,
he slowly passes the smell of my coffee in the Paris Café,
as the blind man comes the opposite way,
swinging his cane hard.

Then seeing him in the evening, along the wide Corniche,
old men with their long poles searching for fish, sidewalk
    soccer matches,
young men on the railing, couples looking out at the hope of it all,
that red ball dropping down again,
filling the countless bullet and shell holes with shadow,
a scarlet tint in their eyes,
the children jumping into water that has taken bodies, raw sewage,
lapped up against fifteen years of civil war.
He drags himself along, slowly, the hard look on his face
is the history of this city, a war that was his entire childhood.

I throw a coin in, a bill, and he doesn't even look up—
he's beyond all such concerns.
Those little bits of clanking metal and squares of painted
    paper portraits
will be converted to food for his mouth,
fuel to drag his body up and down Beirut,
his open can a question
that all their rebuilding can never answer.

FRANK ORTEGA has had work published by *The Madison Review, Colorado Review, Ferro-Botanica, Seneca Review, Z Miscellaneous, Downtown, Amicus Journal* and *Paragraph.* Awards include a Poetry Fellowship from the New York Foundation for the Arts, a performance grant from *Poets & Writers,* as well as various grants to support such projects as a personal film, *What We Hold On To,* that traces three generations of Spanish and American family lines through the use of home movies dating back to the 1920s.

UNDOCUMENTED

My husband calls to say Raffa is in jail. No one is allowed
to see Raffa. The sheriff arrested him, found out he has
no papers. Undocumented, illegal, an immigrant, Raffa is like
my husband. *We're going to have to try to help him,*
my husband says, *have to try to find out what's going on.*
No one knows what's happening, and Raffa doesn't speak
or understand English. *The dumb bastard's been here*
more than twenty years, more than half his life, still doesn't
understand how to speak the language, my husband says
with perverse pride. That was Raffa's choice, but now no one
at the jail knows how to speak Spanish or how to talk to Raffa
(no translator available) and no one on the outside knows
how to talk to the sheriff, who speaks his own language
that has nothing to do with justice or the law. The sheriff tells
my husband even if he pays Raffa's bail, Raffa isn't going
anywhere because the sheriff won't release him. Deportation
looms, and Raffa has no home to go back to. Raffa isn't
allowed to have visitors or make phone calls. Even if he were,
he isn't the type of person to remember phone numbers.
Most of us don't even know each others' real names,
even though we've known each other for years.

AIMEE PARKISON'S story collection, *Woman with Dark Horses,* was published by Starcherone Press. Parkison is currently writing a poetic testimony of her experience of being married to an undocumented immigrant in the U.S. Through her involvement in her husband's plight, Parkison has witnessed many human rights issues, including the cheap and sometimes dangerous labor many immigrants perform, the fear and shame of deportation, the poverty that motivates immigrants to come to America in hopes of providing a better life for their families, and the horror of living in a country where people can be defined as 'illegal,' and the humanity that is lost in the use of that term.

MARK PAWLAK
"PROTECTIVE AND DEFENSIVE DEVICES"

—from a collage by Tuli Kupferberg

In honor of his fourth anniversary as police commissioner, Howard Leary
received a paperweight model of a nightstick from the Mayor.

—New York Daily News

Peerless handcuffs.
Precision American made,
tempered steel, double safety lock, 2 keys.
Model: *Subpoena.*

Leg irons.
Kick proof, pick proof, and run proof.
Model: *Irons.*

Handcuff transport belt.
Restrains prisoner
by keeping hands safely at waist.
Model: *Restrict.*

Twister chain & holder.
Easy to apply;
uses pressure as needed to subdue.
Model: *Safeguard.*

Judo stick.
Unbreakable plastic persuader—defensive item.
Rubber for sure grip.

Used to persuade or subdue the unruly prisoner.
Model: *Judo.*

Midget thumb cuffs.
Off-duty,
especially good for juveniles.
Model: *Spy.*

Aluminum knuckles.
Light cast aluminum,
carries nicely in pocket,
fits hand comfortably.
Model: *Slugger.*

Palm Slapper.
Concealed in palm, powder loaded lead persuader.
Fits easy in pocket.
Model: *Rowdy.*

Lead loaded sap gloves.
Handsome, flexible dress glove
made of genuine Deerskin.
You would never know this is loaded
with 6 oz. powdered lead saps, built-in.
Black only.
Model: *Saboteur.*

MARK PAWLAK is the author of five poetry collections, most recently, *Official Versions*. His work has appeared in *The Best American Poetry*, among many other anthologies and journals, and has been translated into German, Polish, and Spanish. He has received two Massachusetts Artist Fellowship awards. He co-edits *Hanging Loose* magazine. Pawlak has been an antiwar activist since the late '60s and has worked on behalf of equality, social justice and human rights.

NATALIE PEETERSE

MERCADO ORIENTAL

Pablito has a baby food jar
filled with a yellow glue
meant for sealing the soles of shoes
tight his mouth fits tight
over the mouth of the jar he breathes
         in and sighs out
folding himself
into an unused stall
near the trash with the other boys
in a pair of dusted red shorts he'll doze
the ground heavy on his skin
sometimes Pablito will leave
for home sometimes he will wander
the city *una cordoba porfa*
heading to the Palacio Nacional sometimes
         Pablito will go away
with a traveler who likes boys
with an aid
         worker who saves boys
sometimes he will run
errands for change
sometimes if he   breathes enough
         he lopes forward
toward a horizon that must have curves
where she is waiting   she has told him
so many things he remembers but
can't figure   during Purísima she said

the same thing all of the nights—
       he stuns you by degrees

     •

through the rickety charge of stalls
       plastic sandals, yards of tarp to protect
from the late afternoon rain
perfumes, small paper packets of downers
speed and Viagra   malaria pills
rows of bottled rum   Flor de Caña   Ron Plata
men delicately swaying with a few pesos and
old plastic water bottles to be refilled
with clear and treacherous moonshine   *tiyacan*

     •

fresh flowers, avocados
platanos frying   pitaya fruits   limes
the north in abundance not one
coffee bean but tin cans of instant
sugar, brown in big crystals
a man in heavy black
eyeliner and a   black lace top
selling pantyhose and dresses
sings *cosas bonitas para tí, muchachita*
to a girl   pleated blue school uniform
headed for the barrels
of rice and beans, chilies
with two dollar bills in a fist
and Pablito follows the narrow
passageways

                    newly carved meat
a sweetness, warmth and a slight wind
his sandals flip up the freshly
                    washed cement floors   of blood

                              •

the bus is seatless and everyone is balanced
from the one metal bar in the middle of the floor
where the women hold on tightly   children below
their arms   everyone else holds onto an arm that holds onto
an arm that holds the bar in the middle of the bus
driver tears down   half-moons the Rotundo
Santo Domingo and heads
to the Oriental   express
            in the passenger seat a bucket
strapped in   a tube sealed through the cover
with silver tape   coming from the top
            and out the glassless windshield
Pablito is asked to buy gum in the bus lot   pink coconut candy balls
there are Belmonts   matches five more pesos
the noise of other children and
engines   he is the high whine of a cab or the driver or the *chisme*
that passes between the women   only the *entonce* audible
as they wait to sell rocking chairs, mattresses   he is
bright flowered towels, TVs, barrettes and shampoos, aluminum
pots, yellow plastic cups and plates   he is iced bottles
of Coke, Fanta   older boys hustling
bootleg tapes and CDs   saving up for a new pair of fake Tommys
a baseball hat   nothing with a cowboy
brim like Sandino's   Pablito
            blare of horn   the numbness

heat and turpentine he
  is a tendril
breathing at the same pace together
   in the ring the soot the sun
    stand open
he walks out onto the field the sun
   it is just him   and the sky
shoulder blades brittle a breathing
    false thing

NATALIE PEETERSE has an M.F.A. from the University of Montana. Her poetry has appeared in *CutBank: 30th Anniversary Edition*, *Blackbird* and *Sonora Review*, among other journals and anthologies. She has been a fellow with the Arizona Commission on the Arts, a participant at the Squaw Valley Community of Writers, and was most recently an artist-in-residence at the Caldera Institute in central Oregon. She wrote "Mercado Oriental" after living, studying and volunteering in Nicaragua in the fall of 1998.

BENJAMIN L. PÉREZ

AMOUNT:

100,000,000,000,000,000,000,000,
000,000,000,000,000,000,000,000,
000,000,000,000,000,000,000,000,
000,000,000,000,000,000,000,000,
000,000,000,000,000,000,000,000,
000,000,000,000,000,000,000,000,
000,000,000,000,000,000,000,000,
000,000,000,000,000,000,000,000,
000,000,000,000,000,000,000,000,
000,000,000,000,000,000,000,000,
000,000,000,000,000,000,000,000,
000,000,000,000,000,000,000,000,
000,000,000,000,000,000,000,000,
000,000,000,000,000,000,000,000,
000,000,000,000,000,000,000,000,
000,000,000,000,000,000,000,000,
000,000,000,000,000,000,000,000,
000,000,000,000,000,000,000,000,
000,000,000,000,000,000,000,000,
000,000,000,000,000,000,000,000,
000,000,000,000,000,000,000,000.10

COMMANDER AND CHIEF ACKNOWLEDGES RECEIPT OF
SERVICEMEN AND THE GOOD FIGHT IN THE AMOUNT OF
THE TOTAL SHOWN HEREON AND AGREES TO PERFORM THE
OBLIGATIONS SET FORTH BY THE COMMANDER AND CHIEF'S
AGREEMENT WITH THE ISSUER

THANK YOU FOR UTILIZING THE VICE PRESIDENCY

X_____

TOP COPY—MERCHANT
BOTTOM COPY—CUSTOMER

BENJAMIN L. PÉREZ served as a medic in a Combat Engineer unit in the National Guard during the first Gulf War, and though not deployed himself, the experience nonetheless had a profound effect on him: he became a conscientious objector, participated in many of the mass demonstrations against the war that took place in the San Francisco Bay area, and was summarily discharged as a C.O. from the military. As a U.S. History and English instructor at Ex'pression College for Digital Arts he continues the struggle in a more subtle way: by helping his students better hone their critical thinking and analytical skills. His experimental and transgressive work, *The Evil Queen: A Pornolexicology*, was published by Spuyten Duyvil Press.

RHONDA PETTIT

ENFANT TERRIBLE

After their bodies,
one by sweaty one,
collapse onto mine in the brothel, they walk away
mistaking relief for freedom.

They do not know
they must mother me now.
I have made these men pregnant
with their secret.
I am

the secret
they carry like a nine-pound fetus—
unavoidable
unabortable
never born.

We share the same blood,
same word into image.
We pulse.

I am always
full-term and growing. I roll
and kick, wake them from their sleep
in the bed, on the street,
over dinner with the family,
or while shopping for a new suit.

They need it loose.
They need to let out their belts
to contain me.

Multitudes contain me.
Some will carry me by the dozens.
Some will think
they forget

the sweetness, the light,
the thing they have made:
this new life.

RHONDA PETTIT, Ph.D. is an associate professor of English and affiliate faculty of Women's Studies at the University of Cincinnati Raymond Walters College, where she has been using 'Human Rights and the Arts' as a topic for writing and literature courses. Her poetic drama about sex slavery, *The Global Lovers*, was given a staged reading at the Aronoff Center in Cincinnati in 2009. She has published two books on the work of Dorothy Parker—*A Gendered Collision* (2000) and *The Critical Waltz* (2005)—and is a contributing editor to the *Aunt Lute Anthology of U.S. Women Writers, Volumes 1 and 2*.

CLAIRE KAGEYAMA-RAMAKRISHNAN

PERSPECTIVES ON PEOPLE OF JAPANESE AND AMERICAN DESCENT

1. Cruel Irish Jokes, Catholic School, 1980

What's yellow and sleeps alone?
  Yoko Ono.

  What's yellow and rots alone?
    A dead Jap.

2. After Pearl Harbor: Going to Manzanar Relocation Camp

I remember our father taken by the F.B.I.,
  our mother hospitalized.
    We were about to be separated—
Hiro and I with the Ikebuchi family,

Hideo with the Ida family.
  Your father, five years old,
    didn't want to go—
He cried hysterically

 when the Idas put him in the car.
   Hiro ran out and shouted,
    Hey, you can't take him!
He said this in Japanese.

(So the Ikebuchis agreed to take Hideo.)

We couldn't speak English
until we were older.
That was a traumatic
time for your father—

It was for all of us.

3. Survivor of Hiroshima

There were blood stains
and splinters—bone shards
like knives from
my thigh. Scalp
and hair
flapping,
heads with
missing faces.
Carotid artery
without
shoulder
or heart. Cut cheek
in need of stitches.
Split entrails. Lost
fingers, yards from
the live hand.

4. Student at UCLA, 1950

I was a squadron leader—
Japanese kamikaze pilot.
I turned back, (the last mission),
knowing I should fight

to my death.
   Can you blame me
for wanting to live?
   How could I leave
with family in California?
   It was enough I had to urinate
on packages the children
   sent from the States.

5. Nisei on Japanese School

West Los Angeles, 1939

We made "Immon-bukuros,"
   care packages with seaweed and rice,
soy sauce and sugar. We were young

and believed our teacher.

We saved foil from gum
   and cigarette wrappers.
We sang songs for

the strong Japanese soldiers,

shaped the foil into balls.
   We gave our scrap metal—
toy airplanes and trucks

so Japan could make bullets.

6. Person From Japan to a Camp Survivor

Our cities—bombed and flattened.
  We lived like scavengers

looking for food, clean water,
  wood chips to burn, chew.

In camp you had enough to eat,
  a place to sleep.

Do you know what it's like
  to lose your friend?

I walked with my best friend—
  watched an American plane

blow him apart.

CLAIRE KAGEYAMA-RAMAKRISHNAN earned an M.F.A. in Poetry from the University of Virginia, completed her M.A. in Literature at the University of California at Berkeley, and earned a Ph.D. in Literature and Creative Writing from the University of Houston. She is a full-time instructor at Houston Community College, Central Campus. Her second book, *Bear, Diamonds and Crane*, will be published by Four Way Books in 2011. She lives in Houston with her husband, Raj, a scientist specializing in HIV/AIDS research at Baylor College of Medicine, and their three cats.

LOIS RED ELK

NOT ALL GHOSTS ARE DEAD

some still move secretly among Indian homes
waiting for the proper time to release rage. A
kind of rage that builds and overcomes, taking
over all human sense. One minute it is calm, the
women remembering the childhood of playing of
laughing, of merry voices, but growing to loud, the
present turning shades of darkness. Dark pages
begin to call up distant circles in the women's
eyes, spinning from past to present until hearts
beat out of control. They begin reliving all the
beatings over and over. Finally, that secret little
scream, bloodied and stifled since those terrible
childhood times, slips out again for what they had
hoped was the last time. This present laughter
that is so unbearable has to stop like the time
nuns whirled into the room with hairbrushes,
rulers and straps, beating little brown skin, little
fingers and little exposed cheeks, exposure hurting
as bad as the repeated lifting of holy white hands
coming down constantly, down on little Indian girls
for singing, sharing, speaking and being all they
ever knew. But the rage doesn't stop there, it
merges when it is least expected. Now the adult
children of the children have identified and can
control the cruel rush after the laughter, but they
never knew when fear took the place of what was
lost—how to cry, how to trust, how to pray—
never knew why they took up the beating, when

they became the inheritors of the strange catechism.
The women are too old now to be beaten, but they
wonder when the haunting will stop. They wait
somewhere below god, below ancient burial
scaffolds, below crosses, asking the ghosts of nuns
to release the souls of the pitiful little school girls,
those who have suffered the torture long enough.

LOIS RED ELK is an Adjunct Professor at Fort Peck Community
College, Wolf Point, Montana where she has created curriculum on
various Native American cultural topics. She is descended from the
Isanti, Hunkpapa and Ihanktonwan bands of Sioux.

SUSAN RICH

MOHAMUD AT THE MOSQUE

—to my student upon his graduation

And some time later in the lingering
blaze of summer, in the first days
after September 11th you phoned—

if I don't tell anyone my name I'll
pass for an African American.
And suddenly, this seemed a sensible solution—

the best protection: to be a black man
born in America, more invisible than
Somali, Muslim, asylum seeker—

Others stayed away that first Friday
but your uncle insisted that you pray.
How fortunes change so swiftly

I hear you say. And as you parallel
park across from the Tukwila
mosque, a young woman cries out—

her fears unfurling beside your battered car
Go back where you came from!
You stand, both of you, dazzling there

in the mid-day light, her pavement
facing off along your parking strip.
You tell me she is only trying

to protect her lawn, her trees,
her untended heart—already
alarmed by its directive.

And when the neighborhood
policeman appears, asks
you, asks her, asks all the others—

So what seems to be the problem?
He actually expects an answer,
as if any of us could name it—

as if perhaps your prayers
chanted as this cop stands guard
watching over your windshield

during the entire service
might hold back the world
we did not want to know.

SUSAN RICH has received awards from the Academy of American Poets Greenwall Fund and PEN USA. Her books include *The Alchemist's Kitchen; The Cartographer's Tongue: Poems of the World;* and *Cures Include Travel,* all published by White Pine Press. Rich's poems appear in *The Antioch Review, Poetry Ireland Review,* and *New England Review.* A former Fulbright Fellow, Rich has also worked as a staff person for Amnesty International, Oxfam America and the International Red Cross. She lives in Seattle, Washington and teaches at Highline Community College.

NICHOLAS SAMARAS

NIKOSIAN

His Eminence said, Stay for breakfast, but I wanted to walk.

Moments down the path, tank mortars smashed behind me
   into the palace.

I was standing still and running back.

I broke across the fetch—wind moving—everything in slow motion—
   saw
a guard shot, his blood stippled against the white presidential wall
      like impressionist art.

My legs ran.
I hid in lemon groves till their vitamin light drained away.

I moved north by shards of mooncast.
I pulled the earth over me and slept by day.

Then, the invasion came everywhere.

I was awakened by a tapping gun muzzle against my ribcage,
   and taken.

A stolen home. A stolen room.

They left me in a stark cell swept bare of its furniture, its life.

I heard thumping and thumping. Someone crying, walls away.

I pieced together the faintest, muffled invocations in the next room.

The hours were worse when the crying stopped.

The door to my room barked open. We don't speak of this.

What day was it, next?
Without words, they dragged me outside into a dusty sun,
    and let me go.

I walked slowly to a town for water.

When there began a light rain, I believed in God.

NICHOLAS SAMARAS won the Yale Series of Younger Poets Award with his first book. He is from Patmos, Greece and was brought in exile to be raised in America. He has lived in Greece, England, Wales, Switzerland, Austria, Yugoslavia, and Jerusalem. He served as a ghost writer and editor for The Ugandan Democratic Party in Exile, 1974-81, against the political reign of Idi Amin, and works on the ongoing struggle for human rights concerning Cyprus and Serbia. His successive work has appeared or is forthcoming in *The New Yorker, Poetry, The New York Times, New Republic,* and *Kenyon Review.*

WILLA SCHNEBERG

YOU KNOW THE KILLING FIELDS

—for Rada Long, interpreter

She believes because I am Jewish
I must understand
what she went through after Cambodia
was ground down to zero on April 17, 1975,
when grim-faced teenage boys
wearing fatigues over black pajamas,
grenades, pistols, rifles, rockets
weighing down their shoulders,
marched cocky into Phnom Penh.

I must understand how the Angka found her
in the paddies in the moonlight stuffing rice kernels
into her pockets to keep from starving
and bashed in the back of her head with a shovel.

I must understand that they frisked her,
found the eyeglasses inside her *krama*
and smashed them into the monsoon-soaked soil, raving:
*Traitor, intellectual relic, you can't run from
the "Super Great Leap Forward"* and then slashed
her arms with the shards of broken glass.

I must understand why they threatened
to cut out her tongue for humming
a snatch of song sung by Sin Samouth,
the Frank Sinatra of Kampuchea,

who is nothing more to them
than a bourgeois capitalist pig
masquerading as a Frog.

I do not tell her I wasn't there,
that I read about the Holocaust like any goy
who wishes to understand.
Instead, I tell her about a Nazi who sat at a table
covered with delicacies and booze,
holding an automatic pistol in his hand,
who forced Jews to lie naked face down in a pit
and between shots of cognac shot them dead . . .
as if it were my story.
She says, *You don't know how happy
you make me, you know the killing fields.*

WILLA SCHNEBERG received the Oregon Book Award for Poetry for her second collection, *In The Margins Of The World.* From 1992-1993, she worked with the United Nations Transitional Authority (UNTAC) in Cambodia during the first 'free and fair' elections since the French Colonial Period, as a District Electoral Supervisor setting up registration sites in Phnom Penh, and then as a Medical Liaison Officer, providing counseling and arranging repatriation for UN volunteers from member countries. *Storytelling in Cambodia*, her third volume of poetry (Calyx Books, 2006), was inspired by that experience.

WARREN SLESINGER

VAPOR

Vapor (vay.por) n-s. 1. Something
in the air: a mixture of suspended matter
that makes it difficult to see down a street
in Baghdad. 2. A mist with a man in it.

Vaporize (vay.por.ize) v. 1. Only
to convert into a vapor with the heat
mess of manhood high-strung on hate.

Vaporous (vay.por.us) adj. 1. What
is collecting in a cloud of Middle-Eastern
malice. 2. Rising from a blast of body
parts on the same old ground.

WARREN SLESINGER was a university press editor for several
years. He teaches at the University of South Carolina-Beaufort and
belongs to a Unitarian Fellowship with a focus on human relations
and human rights. His poems have appeared in numerous magazines.
He received a poetry fellowship from South Carolina in 2003. *A Word
for It,* a collection of his 'definitions' was published by Finishing Line
Press in 2007.

TRANSLATED BY CAROLYNE WRIGHT WITH THE AUTHOR,

EUGENIA TOLEDO

THE OVEN

—to the city of Temuco

Every night we heard the shots
On Ñielol peak and the surrounding countryside.
It was a winged sound collapsing
As in a poem or a movie about war.
Parrots, *copihue* flowers, and ants
Were dying of fear
Right in the center of Temuco
Surrealistically marked.
Through these beloved streets
Neruda, Mistral, Teillier and others
Had walked writing their verses.
Meanwhile, students were killing themselves with grief
Or they showed up already dead
In the doorways of their houses.

It was the start of the scattering.
The universities dismantled
The radio's daily summonses to present ourselves at the *cuartel*
Set our nerves on edge.
No book to cling to. They outlawed
The Underdogs by Mariano Azuela,
Broad and Alien is the World by Ciro Alegría,
Muriátegui, Cortázar, Manuel Rojas and other writers
Expunged from my classes.

That year even spring fled from Temuco
And letters were delayed who knows how long in arriving.
Ñielol peak had only one deity: the fall.
To go on living was a kind of agony,
A gradual dying of inhaled gas.

EUGENIA TOLEDO was born in Temuco, Chile. After the 1973 military coup that destroyed the government of Salvador Allende, she came to the U.S. to pursue a Ph.D. in Latin American Literature at the University of Washington, married and remained in Seattle with her husband and son. Among her many publications are two books of poetry: *Arquitectura de ausencias/Architecture of Absences* (Editorial Torremozas, España, 2006) and *Tiempo de metales y volcanes/Time of Metals and Volcanoes* (Editorial 400 Elefantes, Nicaragua, 2007). Toledo teaches creative writing and literature at Richard Hugo House, and produces literary and arts events in the Seattle area as a part of the multi-cultural activist organization "*Más allá de una lengua/Beyond One Language.*

ERIC TORGERSEN
VILLANELLE OF THE FINAL REPORT

I don't want the bodies of my kids and a lie,
said one of the mothers who stood by the palace door.
I want to know who killed them, and why.

The country was besieged by a huge and hidden army,
said the government's final report on the 'dirty war.'
Take, eat, it said, these bodies and this lie.

One top Western diplomat told me
he thought the armed forces were trying to shore
up their ranks by not saying who killed, exactly, or why.

Not 'autonomous right wing death squads,' but policy,
said the leading human rights activist, mourning a daughter.
They'd given him nothing to bury except the lie.

A former wellplaced policeman who ran away
called it a pact of blood among young officers.
This seems to answer one question, but not why.

Unless the killers are judged, what happened here yesterday,
the mother continued, will happen tomorrow elsewhere.
Alive in our bodies, elsewhere, we ponder the lie
and the fear of knowing exactly who killed them, and why.

ERIC TORGERSEN is Professor Emeritus of English at Central Michigan University. His most recent book is the novella, *The Man Who Loved Rilke,* March Street Press. At the time of the Vietnam War he co-founded and -edited *Poems of the People,* which distributed political poetry to the underground press.

PRABHAKAR VASAN

TERROR

> ... the world of objects erroneously appears.
>
> —*Asvaghosha*

But still it *does* appear: the sparrow

(tiny body)

trapped in the crawl space.

•

Or a day that, like every other, began with clarity:
the gauze of morning fog unraveling, petals
swirling in the field I know by heart.

I cracked a shutter for light, unhinged
a window for air, admitted this—

Butchered While They Danced—

the front page flapping on the porch.

(wing, broken)

And I took it in:

(injured thing)

(object, hence)

(erroneous)

(but still)

teenagers, a discotheque, bodies and shards,

(still)

the bomber's martyrdom, the minister's assurance
of retaliation, measures of security to be taken.

(a tiny body)

(stirring)

And the eye, in a moment, had its petals again,
the mind its familiar field, again.

(a trapped thing)

(flapping)

(stirring decades
of dust to a frenzy)

And the story was a story among stories.

(the foreign body)

(having found
the way in)

But still, the breath had caught. Something had
lodged in the windpipe, in the airshaft, something

(in the crawl space)

that should have lain in my hand, inert.

(having taken)

(wing)

•

The world appears before we know the world

(all of it)

(the ten thousand petals and shards of it)

is error.

(error)

(but still)

(the offending body)

(appeared)

There is never time to turn from the light,

(the offending bodies)

never time to draw the shutters.

(appear)

PRABHAKAR VASAN works with disenfranchised populations in a community-based social service agency in New York. His poetry and prose have appeared in the journals *6x6, Tarpaulin Sky,* and *Tricyle: The Buddhist Review.* He is currently working on a collection of poems tentatively titled, *Sutures are Sweeter.*

TRANS

I. Learning to be a boy

The neighbor boys look for frogs in the yard. I do not want them to find one. I want them to invent the game in which they are not looking for something to harm. I want them to invent the game in which they are not building villages they will bomb from their plastic planes. They make the bomb noises in unison. They fall down giggling in the grass until their mother names what has been cooking inside.

II. Leaving the house as a man

I was sixteen the first time I saw a drag show. The first time I understood what it meant to "pass," to "appear" and how that "appearing" was a kind of being. It was, as it turned out, my first time in a tie if we don't count the endless number of times I tried on my father's ties in the master bedroom, pulling each one close to my neck trying to learn how to loop the fabric, how to become a man. Here, in this gay bar off the coast of suburban Long Island, drag queens called me "handsome," giggled when I pulled out their chairs and lit their cigarettes. And when I arrive home late, when I try to sneak in through the back sliding glass door, my mother sees me in the suit and tie. She, for a moment, covers her eyes as though I had been naked and not her child. "What are you doing?" she wants to know. "Where could you have gone dressed like that?"

III. The chalk of androgyny

There was always something about the public bathroom doors, always the chalk of androgyny sticking in my throat as I'd walk towards the women's room with my mother. She wasn't bothered by the stick figure triangle skirt that indicated the path we were to take, the ways we were to interpret our bodies. But my mother and I do not have the same body. We do not read the signs on the bathroom doors in the same way. My mother does not read the doors at all; she is automatic in her automatic body. She tugs me in by my small arms and leads me to the stall. Often, I have trouble urinating. I ask my mother to sing so no one will hear my body and she does. "I'm leavin' on a jetplane, don't know when I'll be back again . . . leavin' on a jetplane, don't know when I'll be back again."

IV. Praying for gender

Then there is my crying in dresses. "Since I was born," my mother says. She walks the line of my crying. The church dress I will not. The pigtails I will not. The long nights praying: *Please God, if you let me wake up and be a boy, I will never say another swear word again.*

V. An imposition of meaning

Naming. Kindergarten. I do not like salt water, the class gerbil or writing on the black board. I do not like the girls' line and the boys' line. I do not like swallowing my gum. I will not tell anyone my middle name. The teacher, she tells the whole class my middle name. "It's Ann," they scream, "we know it's Ann."

"Don't count on it"—was what my father used to say to mean *no*. The trees never mean it. They spit up fire. They sometimes think they can make stars. No one is there to deny them.

STACEY WAITE has published two collections of poems: *Choke* (winner of the 2004 Frank O'Hara Prize in Poetry) and *Love Poem to Androgyny* (winner of the 2006 Main Street Rag Chapbook Competition). Her poems have been published most recently in *Bloom, The Marlboro Review, Gulf Stream, Nimrod* and *Poet Lore. The Lake Has No Saint* is forthcoming from Tupelo Press in 2010. Stacey has also taught workshops and diversity trainings related to gender multiplicity and queer youth in local high schools and colleges in Pennsylvania, West Virginia and Ohio.

BRIDGET WHEARTY

FOR THOSE WHO REMIND ME DAILY THAT MY RIGHTS, SUCH AS THEY ARE, ARE A WRONG AND SELFISH FIGHT

How are you different
from the ones who say 'no,'
the ladies in peony-flowered dresses and pinching shoes,
rising
on every Sunday
like the Sunday before?

March 4th and paper
shifts in the bus stop's corners—
like old leaves, or the whisper of thigh against thigh—
and Susan Thompson says to a sympathetic reporter,
"It's not that I judge them,
but they shouldn't get married."

In the rooms of your eyes,
I am dismembered—
my mouth here, my hands there,
the burn mark on my wrist that should have healed but didn't.
You measure my politics
and past, and by the gleam in your eyes
as you lift your glass
I know I have been found wanting.

Not queer enough, you tell me.
I am fighting for the wrong things,

but I have not even been fighting.
In your balance, O God of Judgment,
another mark of my shame.

What is this longing for marriage?
It is true, the words of the state,
purchased paper
with a printed frame—
an expensive incantation
against dying alone.

Against your words,
and Mrs. Thompson's fervor,
I am less than nothing.
A feather in the balance,
a puff of selfish air.

In her Apocalypse, your Revolution—
I am the soil-gazing apostate:
satisfied with cooking,
I have failed you both.
In the sun, in the evening,
God and Anarchy pale
against steel and sage
in my lover's moving hands.

BRIDGET WHEARTY was born in Helena, Montana. She began working for Lesbian, Gay, Bisexual, and Transgender (LGBT) rights following the 2002 arson of a lesbian couple's home in Missoula and has worked on LGBT rights initiatives in Montana, Texas, and California. In 2003, she graduated from the University of Montana with a B.A. in Creative Writing and English Literature. She is currently a student in the English Literature Ph.D. program at Stanford University, and lives in the Bay Area with her wife.

INTERROGATION II

—after the painting by Leon Golub

(Four interrogators; a victim, bound and hooded; red walls, a ladder-like device with chain; a chair)

1.

There will always be an issue: doctrine, dogma, differences of con-
science, politics, or creed.
There will always be a reason: heresy, rebellion, dissidence, inadequate
conviction or compliance.

There will always be the person to command it: president or king, dic-
tator or chief of staff,
and the priest or parson to anoint it, consecrate it, bless it, ground its
logic in the sacred.

There will always be the victim; trembling, fainting, fearful, abducted,
bound, and brought here;
there will always be the order, and the brutes, thugs, reptiles, scum, to
carry out the order.

There will always be the room, the chair, the room whose walls are
blood, the chair of shame.
There will always be the body, hooded, helpless; and the soul within,
trembling, fearful, shamed.

2.

If I am here, hooded, helpless,
within these walls of blood,

upon this chair of shame,
something had to think me here.

I lived within my life,
I only thought my life,

I was stolen from it:
something *thought* me from it.

If something thought me,
there had to be a mind,

and if there was a mind,
it had to be contained, revealed,

as I thought mine was,
within a strip of temporal being.

If it was another mind,
like mine, that thought

and bound and brought me here,
some other consciousness

within its strip of being,
didn't it, that bit of being,

have to feel as I must feel
the nothingness against it,

the nothingness encroaching
on the rind of temporality,

the strand of actuality,
in which it is revealed?

Wasn't it afraid
to jeopardize the sensitivity

with which it knows itself,
with which it senses being

trembling upon nothingness,
struggling against nothingness,

with which it holds away
the nothingness within itself

which seems to strive to join
into that greater void?

When it stole me from my life,
abducted me and bound me,

wouldn't it have felt itself
being lost within the void

of nothingness within it?
Wasn't it afraid?

3.

Why are you crying?
Nothing is happening.

No one is being tortured,
no one beaten.

Why are you crying?
Nothing is happening.

No one's genitals nails spine
crushed torn out shattered.

No one's eardrums burst with fists,
no one's brain burst with bludgeons.

Why are you crying?
Nothing is happening.

No one's bones unsocketed
fractured leaching marrow.

No one flayed, flogged, maimed,
seared with torches,

set afire racked
shot electrocuted hung.

Why are you crying?
Nothing is happening.

There is only a chair,
a room, a ladder,

flesh indelibly marked
with pain and shame.

Why are you crying?
Nothing is happening.

4.

The human soul, the soul
we share, the single soul,

that by definition
which is our essential being,

is composed of other souls,
inhabited by other beings:

thus its undeniable power,
its purity, its vision,

thus its multiplicity
in singularity,

I understand the composition
of the soul, its communality,

but must I share my soul
with brutes and reptiles,

must I share my being,
vision, purity, with scum?

Impossible that in the soul
the human species

should be represented
as these brutes and thugs;

mortal substance
bodied as these reptiles.

Soul would loathe itself,
detest its very substance,

huddle in its lurk of essence
howling out its grief

of temporality, snarling out
its rage of mutability,

rather than be represented
by these beasts of prey.

The human soul is being
devoured by beasts of prey.

The human soul is prey.

5.

I didn't know the ladder to divinity on which were dreamed ascending
          and descending angels,
on which sodden spirit was supposed to rarify and rise, had become an
          instrument of torment,

wrist-holes punctured in its rungs, chains to hold the helpless body
        hammered in its uprights.

I didn't know how incidental life can seem beside such implements of
        pain and degradation;
neither did I know, though, how much presence can be manifested in
        the hooded, helpless body:
brutalized and bound, sinews, muscles, skin, still are lit with grace and
        pride and hope.

We cry from shame, because the body and the soul within are mocked,
        displayed, and shamed.
There will always be a reason, there will always be a victim, rooms of
        blood, chairs of pain.
But will there be the presence, grace and hope and pride enduring
        past the pain and shame?

C.K. WILLIAMS is the author of numerous books of poetry, in-
cluding *Collected Poems* (Farrar, Straus, and Giroux, 2006), *The Singing,*
(2003), which won the National Book Award; *Repair* (1999), winner
of a Pulitzer Prize; *The Vigil* (1997); *A Dream of Mind* (1992); *Flesh and
Blood* (1987), which won the National Book Critics Circle Award;
Tar (1983); *With Ignorance* (1997); *I Am the Bitter Name* (1992); and
Lies (1969). Among his many awards and honors are an American
Academy of Arts and Letters Award, a Guggenheim Fellowship, the
Lila Wallace-Reader's Digest Award, the PEN/Voelcker Award for
Poetry, and a Pushcart Prize. Williams teaches in the Creative Writing
program at Princeton University, and lives part of each year in Paris.

CAROLYNE WRIGHT

KZ

Arbeit Macht Frei

—motto over the entrance of every Nazi concentration camp

We walk in under the empty tower, snow
falling on barbed-wire nets where the bodies
of suicides hung for days. We follow signs
to the treeless square, where the scythe blade, hunger,
had its orders, and some lasted hours in the cold
when all-night roll calls were as long as winter.

We've come here deliberately in winter,
field stubble black against the glare of snow.
Our faces go colorless in wind, cold
the final sentence of their bodies
whose only identity by then was hunger.
The old gate with its hated grillework sign

walled off, we take snapshots to sign
and send home, to show we've done right by winter.
We've eaten nothing, to stand inside their hunger.
We count, recount crimes committed in snow—
those who sheltered their dying fellows' bodies
from the work details, the transport trains, the cold.

Before the afternoon is gone, the cold
goes deep, troops into surrendered land. Signs
direct us to one final site, where bodies
slid into brick-kiln furnaces all winter

or piled on iron stretchers in the snow
like a plague year's random harvest. What hunger

can we claim? Those who had no rest from hunger
stepped into the ovens, knowing already the cold
at the heart of the flame. They made no peace with snow.
For them no quiet midnight sign
from on high—what pilgrims seek at the bottom of winter—
only the ebbing measure of their lives. Their bodies

are shadows now, ashing the footprints of everybody
who walks here, ciphers carrying the place of hunger
for us, who journey so easily in winter.
Who is made free by the merciless work of cold?
What we repeat when we can't read the signs—
the story of our own tracks breaking off in snow.

Snow has covered the final account of their bodies
but we must learn the signs: they hungered,
they were cold, and in Dachau it was always winter.

CAROLYNE WRIGHT has published eight books and chapbooks of poetry, four collections of poetry in translation from Spanish and Bengali, a volume of essays, and most recently *Majestic Nights: Love Poems of Bengali Women* (White Pine Press, 2008). Wright's year in Chile during the presidency of Salvador Allende was life-changing: many whom she knew during that time died, disappeared, or went into exile after the 1973 military coup supported by the U.S. government. She has taught for social service organizations, women's centers, prison workshops, and done other outreach work to connect with marginal and underserved communities within the U.S. and Chile.

WHAT I KNOW IS THE FIGHT

What I know is the fight
the feeling of steel in the mind
and the hollow tunnel of heart
already blown completely clean.

What I know are the neighborhoods
the small towns filled with disfigured dreams
and brains locked from birth.

What I know is the fight
the Indian hands and the white
the Mexican hands and the
thrill that passes through them
when they touch
and when they burn.

ERIKA T. WURTH is a mixed-blood American Indian (Apache/
Chickasaw/Cherokee) poet and fiction writer. Her book, *Indian Trains,*
was published by the University of New Mexico's *West End Press*. Her
work appears or is forthcoming in *Raven Chronicles, Fiction, Pembroke,
Cedar Hill Review, AMCRJ, SAIL, Ellipsis, Boulevard, 5AM, Borderlands,
Global City Review, Bryant Literary Review, Stand* and *Red Ink*. She lives
in Macomb, Illinois where she teaches Creative Writing at Western
Illinois University. Recently, she was a visiting writer at the Institute
of American Indian Arts.

ACKNOWLEDGMENTS

Sandra Alcosser: "The Blue Vein," published by Brighton Press, 2006.

Peter Anderson: An earlier, and therfore somewhat different version of "Key to the Kingdom" appeared in a poetry collection, *Vanishing Ground* (Quartz Press, Johannesburg, 2000).

Ellen Bass: "Bearing Witness" from the book, *Mules of Love,* was published by BOA Editions, 2002.

Joseph Bathanti: "Cletis Pratt" won the 2007 Barbara Mandigo Kelly Peace Poetry Prize, awarded annually by the Nuclear Age Peace Foundation. It has been published in *The Sunflower,* the Nuclear Age Peace Foundation's newsletter, and also in *Solo Cafe.* It was also nominated for a 2008 Pushcart Prize.

Marvin Bell: "Bagram, Afghanistan, 2002" from the book, *Mars Being Red,* was published by Copper Canyon Press, 2007.

Tamiko Beyer: "Report" was previously published in *diode* (Winter 2009, Volume 2, Number 2).

Mark Brazaitis: "The Policeman" originally appeared in *Witness.*

Donna Brook: "Poem Wrapped Around a Quotation from Samantha Power" was published in *Present/Tense: Poets in the World,* an anthology edited by Mark Pawlak (Hanging Loose Press, 2004).

Martha Collins: "Lynch," from the book, *Blue Front,* (Graywolf, 2006). Used by permission of the author and publisher.

Roger Dunsmore: "A True War Story," *Roger Dunsmore's Greatest Hits, 1969-2006,* Pudding House Publications, 2007.

Carolyn Forché: "The Museum of Stones" was first published by *The New Yorker,* March 26, 2007.

Kim Goldberg: "Gates of the City," from the book, *Red Zone,* which will be published in September 2009 by Pig Squash Press.

Christopher Howell: "If the Moon Kept Goats" is scheduled to appear in the next issue of *Prairie Schooner.*

Yusef Komunyakaa: "Surge" from his book, *Warhorses* (Farrar, Straus and Giroux, 2009).

Marilyn Krysl: "Target," first appeared in *Swear the Burning Vow: Selected and New Poems 2009.*

Li-Young Lee: "Self-Help for Fellow Refugees" from the book, *Behind My Eyes* (W.W. Norton, 2008).

Philip Memmer: "Watching the Baby Sleep" from *Threat of Pleasure* (Word Press, 2008). Copyright 2008 by Philip Memmer. Used with permission of the author.

Peter Metres: "Letter to My Sister" was previously published in *Artful Dodge,* and also appears in the collection, *To See the Earth* (2008).

Tiffany Midge: "After Viewing the Holocaust Museum's Room of Shoes and a Gallery of Plains Indian Moccasins: Washington, D.C." was first published in *Cold Mountain Review (*Fall, 2005).

Judith H. Montgomery: "Simmer" was first published in the *Bellingham Review* (Spring, 2006).

Taslima Nasrin: "Noorjahan" was first published in *The Game in Reverse: Poems by Taslima Nasrin* (George Braziller, Inc., 1995). English text (translations, preface and notes) by Carolyne Wright.

Sheryl Noethe: "No Exchange of Livestock," published in the book, *As Is*, by Lost Horse Press (2009).

Frank Ortega: "Beirut" was first published in *Oberon* (Summer 2009), which is published by the Oberon Foundation in Stony Brook, N.Y.

Mark Pawlak: "Protective and Defensive Items" is from the book, *Official Versions* (Hanging Loose Press, 2006).

Natalie Peeterse: "Mercado Oriental" was first published in *Global Human: A Literary E-Journal of International Culture* (Issue 2/August 2008).

Benjamin L. Pérez: "AMOUNT" was published in *Cricket Online Review* (www.cricketonlinereview.com/Volume 3/Number 1).

Susan Rich: "Mohamud at the Mosque" from the book, *Cures Include Travel*, published by White Pine Press in 2006.

Nicholas Samaras: "Nikosia" was published in *Prairie Schooner* (Volume 80, Number 4) by the University of Nebraska.

Willa Schneberg: "You Know the Killing Fields" was previously published in *Americas Review* and *Storytelling in Cambodia,* (Calyx Books, 2006).

Warren Slesinger: "Vapor" was first published in the *Comstock Review,* 2009.

Eugenia Toledo: "The Oven." is forthcoming in *Poetry International,* 2009.

Eric Torgersen: "Villanelle of the Final Report" first appeared in *Ironwood.* It contains a large amount of found material from Martin Andersen's article, "Stones for Bread," *The Nation,* May 14, 1983.

Stacie Waite: "Trans" was first published in *Knockout,* Spring 2009.

C.K. Williams: "Interrogation II" was published in *Collected Poems* (Farrar, Straus and Giroux, 2006).

Carolyne Wright: "KZ" was originally published in *Blood to Remember: American Poets on the Holocaust* (Texas Tech University Press, 1991; 2nd edition, Time Being Books, 2007) and in *Seasons of Mangoes and Brainfire* (Eastern Washington University Press/ Lynx House Books, 2nd edition, 2005).

Erica Wurth: "What I Know is the Fight," was first published in the book, *Indian Trains,* by West End Press.

ABOUT THE EDITORS

MELISSA KWASNY is the author of three books of poetry, *Reading Novalis in Montana, Thistle* and *The Archival Birds,* as well as the editor of *Toward the Open Field: Poets on the Art of Poetry 1800-1950.* She lives in western Montana.

M.L. SMOKER belongs to the Assiniboine and Sioux tribes of the Fort Peck Reservation in northeastern Montana. She holds an M.F.A. from the University of Montana, where she was the recipient of the Richard Hugo Fellowship. She is also a graduate of Pepperdine University, and attended UCLA and the University of Colorado, where she was a Battrick Fellow. Her first collection of poems, *Another Attempt at Rescue,* was published by Hanging Loose Press in 2005. Her poems have also appeared in *Shenendoah, South Dakota Review, Many Mountains Moving* and have been translated for *Acoma,* an Italian literary journal published by the University of Rome. She was recently named Director of Indian Education for the state of Montana.

The editors would like to especially thank Christine Holbert, publisher of Lost Horse Press, for her vision and commitment to human rights, and for giving us the opportunity to work on this book together.